# THE
# KING'S COLLEGE CHOIR
# BOOK

# THE
# KING'S COLLEGE CHOIR
## BOOK

*edited by*

Jonathan Rippon and Penny Cleobury

**Phillimore**

1997

Published by
PHILLIMORE & CO. LTD.
Shopwyke Manor Barn, Chichester, West Sussex

ISBN 1 86077 052 5

Printed and bound in Great Britain by
BUTLER AND TANNER LTD.
London and Frome

# CONTENTS

# LIST OF ILLUSTRATIONS

# FOREWORD

When King Henry VI laid the foundation stone of the Chapel of King's College, Cambridge, in 1446, he was providing for the religious needs of a Provost, seventy fellows and scholars, ten priests, ten chaplains, six clerks (singing men) and sixteen choristers (boys), as later recorded in the statutes of 1453. It was specified that sixteen choristers were to be '… of sound condition and honest conversation'.

Could the King, as he laid the foundation stone, have guessed with confidence that his Chapel would be recognised by successive generations as one of the great architectural glories of the world, described thus by Wordsworth? …

> *Where light and shade repose, where music dwells*
> *Lingering—and wandering on as loth to die;*
> *Like thoughts whose very sweetness yieldeth proof*
> *That they were both for immortality.*

Could the King have envisaged that the successors of his sixteen original boy choristers (still, I hope, of honest conversation!) would, 550 years later, be singing not only to a 'scanty band of white-robed scholars' but to the many thousands who visit his Chapel each year?

It would certainly have been beyond the King's wildest dreams that through the medium of recording, and through radio and television, the sound of the Choir at King's College, Cambridge, should be brought to countless homes in every continent.

This book is intended to give some insight into the lives of the young men and boys who, for a few years of their lives, contribute through their singing to the maintenance of the centuries-old choral tradition so revered by John Milton:

Her Royal Highness The Duchess of Kent, in her capacity as Patron of the Choir Schools' Association, visiting King's College Chapel in April 1993. Photograph: *Cambridge Evening News*.

> *There let the pealing organ blow,*
> *To the full-voiced quire below,*
> *In service high, and anthems clear*
> *As may, with sweetness, through mine ear,*
> *Dissolve me into ecstacies,*
> *And bring all Heaven before mine eyes.*

**HRH The Duchess of Kent**

# PREFACE

Singing in King's College Choir is an experience that no one forgets. Whether at the famous *Festival of Nine Lessons and Carols*, on one of the Choir's regular international tours, at a recording session, a public concert, or at one of the daily services in the magnificent surroundings of the Chapel, being a choral scholar or chorister at King's uplifts you emotionally and spiritually forever.

A chance conversation between the editors on a Bermudian beach, during a Choir tour in January 1995, laid the foundation for this book. The inspiration had come from John Nichols, who was Jonathan Rippon's English tutor at Eton. Its publication coincides with the establishment of the King's College Chapel Foundation, and the celebrations for Boris Ord's centenary.

We wanted to write a book to chronicle a great institution; to provide a glimpse into the life of the Choir for an observer, and to bring back fond memories to everyone who has been directly associated with it. It is intended to provide an outline of the Choir's many activities throughout the year.

We are grateful for the time and generosity of former and present members of the Choir, Chapel clergy and staff, members of King's College and Eton College, and others who have written contributions. Thanks are due also to the many photographers who have given us permission to use their work.

We have tried to give as broad a view as possible of the different eras in the Choir's history, but have naturally been limited by space and the material we had access to. However, we hope the book will bring enjoyment and inspiration to all who read it.

JONATHAN RIPPON
PENNY CLEOBURY

# ACKNOWLEDGEMENTS

Photographs from the College Library and the Rowe Music Library appear by kind permission of the Provost and Fellows of King's College, Cambridge. Many other people have helped to make this book possible. We are grateful to the Syndics of Cambridge University Library, who gave permission for the use of the Loggan prints: Lord Salisbury who generously allowed us to reproduce the portrait of King Henry VI from Hatfield House: *Cambridge Evening News*, Eaden Lilley (Photography) and The Cambridgeshire Collection for their many photographic contributions, and Harpercollins Publishing for consenting to the inclusion of lines from 'Sylvia Plath's Letters Home'.

Particular thanks go to Margaret Cranmer, the Rowe Music Librarian, and Peter Jones, the Librarian of King's College, for their kindness and co-operation, and to Andrew Parker, who has freely shared his encyclopaedic knowledge of the Choir. Our special gratitude goes to Stephen Cleobury for his encouragement and help with proof-reading and to Laura Cleobury, without whose help and many hours at the word-processor this book would not have become a reality. Finally we express our appreciation to the following for their invaluable help, while offering our sincere apologies to those whose names may inadvertently have been omitted:

Mrs. Chris Bagnall
Mr. Ian Barter
Mr. Christopher Bishop
Mr. John Boulter and the Chapel Staff
Miss Irene Seccombe
Ms. Tricia Clarke
Mr. Andrew Corbett
Mr. Hubert Darke
Mr. & Mrs. Simon Eadon
Mrs. Kristina Edwards
Mrs. Peggie Guest
Mr. Robin Harcourt Williams
Mr. James Hossack
The Rev. David Isitt
Mr. Christopher Jakes
Mr. & Mrs. Philip Ledger
Mr. Douglas Morgan
Ms. Gillian Oakley
The Rev. Dr. George Pattison
Mr. & Mrs. Gerald Peacocke
Mr. Robert Satchwell
Mr. Cedric Tarrant
Mrs. Sydney Wilkinson
Sir David & Lady Willcocks
Mr. Rodney Williams

Abbreviations: ch. = chorister; c.s. = choral scholar; c.t. = chorister tutor; o.s. = organ scholar; O. & D. of M. = Organist and Director of Music.

*Chapter One*

# INTRODUCTION

## What is King's College Choir?
### *Penny Cleobury*

King's College Choir, like many other cathedral and collegiate choirs in Britain, is made up of the four main singing voices. The trebles, or sopranos, aged between nine and fourteen years, attend King's College School. This is housed in buildings just across the river from the College and Chapel. The school has some two hundred and eighty girls and boys from nursery age through to fourteen, when they leave for their senior school. The choristers have exactly the same education as the other children; their musical commitments come before and after school hours.

Today the men of the choir, four counter-tenors (altos), four tenors and six basses, are all undergraduates at King's College reading for degrees in many different subjects. They go through a singing audition (choral trial) in late September to become choral scholars, at which they are also interviewed academically.

Choristers, too, have a singing audition (chorister trial). The Director of Music holds this once or twice a year, but he is not expecting perfection at age seven! What he is looking for is lively musicality, while the Headmaster assesses the children's academic potential. All choristers receive scholarships (worth about two-thirds of the school fees), and it is the College's intent to make sure that no child should be barred from singing in the Choir because of financial hardship.

During the week, the choristers have a morning rehearsal with the Director of Music, and then join the men for a full choir rehearsal before Evensong. On Sundays there is also a morning service, but on Mondays there are no sung services. The Chapel services are the *raison d'être* of the Choir, but its members also enjoy the delights of foreign travel and prestigious recordings and concerts.

## King's College Choir History
### *Andrew Parker, c.s. 1968-72*

### An Increasing Audience through Five and a Half Centuries

When King's College was founded in 1441, King Henry VI had the intention that the Choir, which was to provide music for the daily offices and celebrations of the mass, should also afford an educational opportunity for the choristers. The 16 boys were to be 'poor' and 'needy', under the age of 12 at their admission, and they had to be competent to read and sing. They would receive their clothing and teaching as well as any musical instruction. The older members of the musical establishment were to be 10 secular chaplains and six stipendiary lay clerks. From either of these adult categories would be drawn one who was to play the organ.

It would appear that the choir was not established in full until towards the end of the 1440s. For the majority of the time that they sang in the temporary chapel the nature of the music was largely soloistic. A choir would not have had the role of leading the singing which it performs today; the music as an embellishment and perfection of the worship was offered more as a vehicle for meditation, and there was no expectation of any sort that a congregation might participate, if such congregation was present at all.

Composers of English choral music in the second half of the 15th century were beginning to explore the possibilities of sonority. The surviving repertoire from other establishments, during what would have been the first eighty years of the life of the King's College Choir, display structures, in sonic terms, which would at first sight seem entirely wed-ded to the architectural space which the King's College Chapel represents. Yet the irony is that until the eve of the Reformation none of this music may have been sung by the Choir in the Chapel as we know it, since the building took so long to complete, and this sort of singing would probably have been heard only in the far smaller tem-porary building which served as the college chapel until it fell down in 1536.

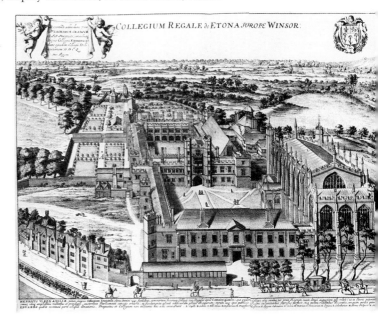

Once the Choir had moved into the new building they were soon beset by the politics of the Reformation, and it was to be well over a century, fol-lowing the Restoration of the monar-chy in 1660, before there was any last-ing stability in the Chapel. Around 1550 the Choir was subject to the dis-banding which many other musical

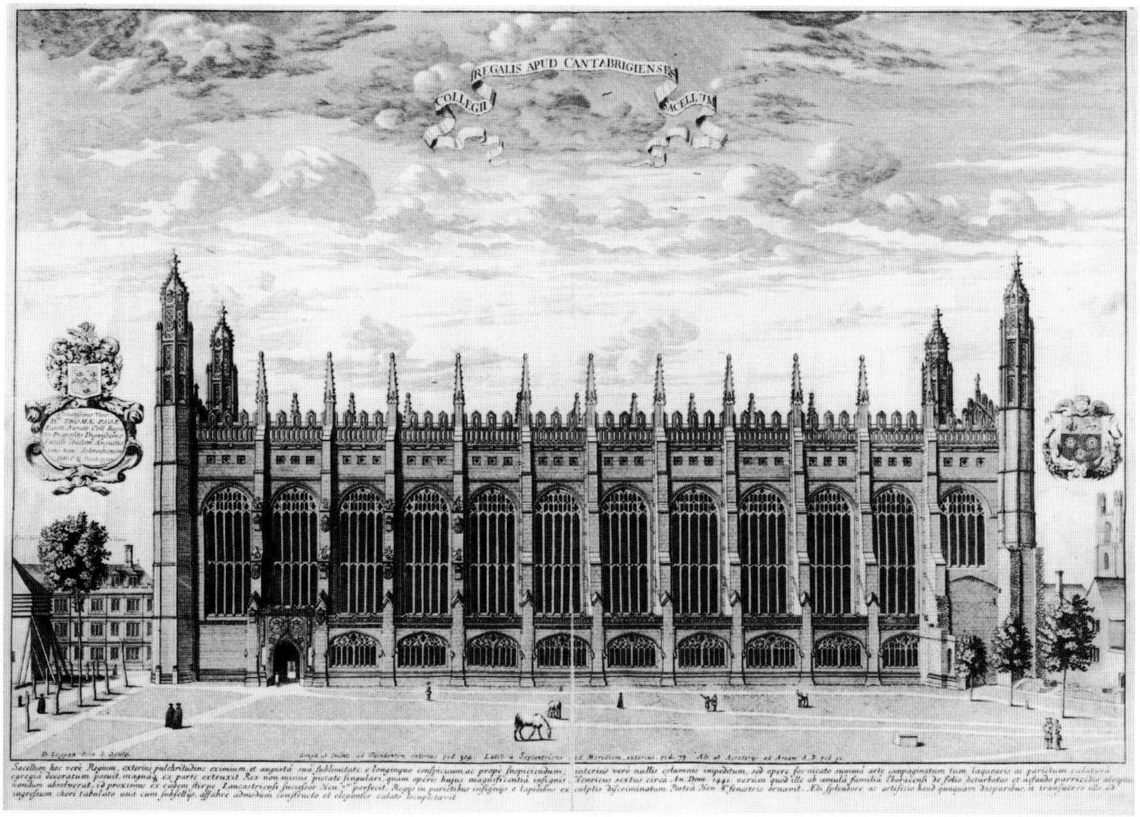
REGALIS APUD CANTABRIGIENSIS
COLLEGII
SACELLUM

**1** (above far left) Founder's Document. At the top of the illumination, the Virgin Mary and St Nicholas, the two patron saints of the College, are shown. Underneath, King Henry VI is depicted, kneeling with members of the House of Lords (above), and members of the House of Commons (below), praying for the prosperity of the College. Photograph: Tim Rawle.

**2** (above left) The Founder, King Henry VI, from a portrait in Hatfield House.

**3** (left) An overall view of Eton College, founded by King Henry VI in 1440: print by David Loggan, *Cantabrigia Illustrata* 1690: Cambridge University Library.

**4** (above) The Chapel, including the old bell-tower (on the left): print by David Loggan, *Cantabrigia Illustrata* 1690: Cambridge University Library.

establishments suffered during the fervour of the Edwardine liturgical reforms. Brought back into existence during the reign of Mary Tudor in 1553-4, perhaps with much of its repertoire for the Catholic liturgy intact, the Choir continued uninterrupted during the many changes and musical strictures which characterised the reign of Queen Elizabeth I. Although the statutes had remained the same since the foundation, there had been since 1559 generally only two chaplains, or 'conducts', and six or seven lay clerks. The organist seems to have been regarded as a separately identifiable person only from 1606. The 1620s was a period of remarkable musical activity in Cambridge, and the Choir flourished from this time until the prohibitions of the Commonwealth forbade new choristers from being recruited from about 1646. By 1652 the Chapel was probably silent. It is thus only after 1660 that the Choir can be said to have sung in the Chapel continuously.

So, once the Choir had settled down, what sort of people filled the choir stalls? The boys were, no doubt, 'poor and needy' in the broadest sense, and they were often sons of servants either in King's College or elsewhere in the university. Occasionally they were sons of lay clerks. The lay clerks themselves might either be college servants, or have some trade in the town. Only later were they involved in independent musical careers. As late as 1799 the back row of the stalls was filled largely with artisans; it was not until the 19th century that the age of the professional lay clerk arrived, and one can observe singers coming from cathedral posts to King's for a few years and then moving on, perhaps in search of a singing career in the growing concert and oratorio world. Unlike the previous century, in the 1800s only a few stayed until retirement, which usually meant until final ill health or death prevented them continuing. Lay clerks were stall-holders for life, whatever the condition of their vocal chords! In addition, the gentlemen of King's

College Choir also acted as lay clerks for Trinity and St John's Colleges, whose services were not so frequent; thus their attention to duty in King's was not exclusive.

In the mid-19th century the spirit of reform visited the University, which was consequently required by parliament to undertake a complete overhaul of its educational function. King's had been, under the Founder's statutes, a body of 70 scholars and fellows. The scholars were elected exclusively from the sister foundation at Eton, and, in turn, they might expect automatically to proceed to a fellowship as one became vacant. The wholesale revision of statutes among all the colleges meant that, from 1861, King's College ceased to be a small, closed society and began the process of opening its doors to an increasing number of undergraduates. In the Choir, too, there began to be changes. The back row was augmented with a number of supernumerary lay clerks who would attend on Sundays and some other festivals. This, in theory (although not, it would seem, in practice), might allow the Choir to perform more elaborate music, but the additional appointments were probably created to help cover the multiple duties around Cambridge which the statutory six lay clerks had to perform. A novelty was the introduction of weekly choir practices: before that time only the boys had, one presumes, rehearsed the music, and the lay clerks would turn up and sing in whichever traditional manner they accustomed themselves to. In the early 1870s Trinity College decided to form their own, independent, choir, with Charles Villiers Stanford, still an undergraduate, as the Organist. Thus the supernumeraries were released, some of whom migrated down the road to Trinity and St John's. One major change was brought about by the establishment of boarding choristers, rather than relying on the offspring of local menials. To begin with they lived in Fitzwilliam House, under the care of one of the Chaplains. With this it became possible to attract a different type of chorister, and many of the first intake in 1875 were sons of professional people, doctors, clergymen and schoolmasters. In 1878 a separate choir school was established in West Road.

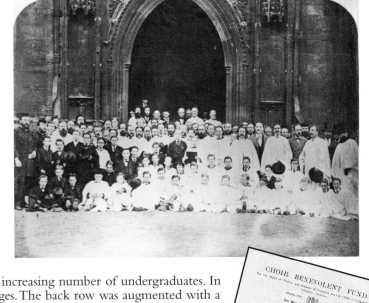

The services in Chapel, too, became more public. Before the late 19th century it had been necessary to have written 'order' from a fellow of the College for any visitor to attend a service in King's. The Chapel was simply not equipped for large congregations: there was little seating, apart from the carved stalls, which were reserved for the different hierarchies of the members of the College. Even as late as the 1890s a curious custom was still observed, of the congregation standing throughout the anthem at Evensong, and earlier prints of the interior of the Chapel, showing visitors perambulating while the Choir sang, might only be reflecting a necessity caused by the lack of seats.

The main change in the musical establishment was to be effected by the appointment in 1876 of Arthur Henry Mann as Organist, at the age of twenty-six. Since 1743 there had been only three organists: John Randall (1743-1799), also Professor of music, John Pratt, his pupil (1799-1855), and William Amps (1855-1876), who also had followed in the master-pupil tradition. The difference with Mann's appointment is that it was held by an open competition. Mann had been a star pupil of Zechariah Buck, renowned Organist of Norwich Cathedral, which

**5** The first known photograph to include the Choir, at a Choral Festival, dated 1873. Photograph: Rowe Library. Also the programme sheet from the festival.

had developed some of the highest standards of musical performance in the country earlier that century. While Mann's task was to bring the Choir to greater musical 'efficiency', as the Victorians liked to call it, he was aided by the well-directed reforming zeal of several of the fellows, who saw the possibility that the entire King's College Choir of the future could become a part of the educational process, now that the College was open to non-Etonians. The lay clerks could initially be augmented, and then replaced, by undergraduate singers, who would hold choral scholarships. Starting in 1880 this was, inevitably, a gradual process, since no lay clerk's contract could be terminated on grounds of intended change, and the method had to be one of 'natural wastage'. The number of choral scholars remained at about four until after World War I, and it was June 1927 before the last of the lay clerks had left the choir stalls.

Mann was encouraged, even kept up to the mark, by some of the musically-inclined fellows. Until Edward Dent became a Fellow in 1902 there were no professional musicians among the dons, and Mann would always regard himself as the sole musical expert in Chapel. He developed for his choir a distinctive sound and manner of singing which suited the reverberation of the building. He took many pieces of music at a slow pace, and his organ-playing exhibited a lusciousness of registration. His choice of repertoire remained, for a long time, unyieldingly Victorian. Although, during his middle years at King's, he was to be persuaded by some of the fellows to widen the scope of the music lists to include pieces which pre-dated the 18th century, and his beloved Handel, the greatest influence on Mann was to come from Eric Milner-White, who returned to King's (having been an undergraduate and, later, Chaplain) as Dean, in 1918.

Milner-White had been persuaded to accept the appointment by M.R. James, the outgoing Provost. James had been lifelong friends with the Benson family, having been a contemporary at Eton with A.C. Benson, and he had frequently visited Truro when Benson's father was Bishop there, before being translated to Canterbury. Monty James therefore knew all about the Truro experiment with a Christmas Eve service as it was taking place in the 1880s, and, together with Milner-White, he probably effected its importation to King's. In December 1918 this became the first of the 'new works' under Milner's decanate. Modified the following year more to the form which would be recognised today, thus the *Festival of Nine Lessons and Carols* was born.

**6** The first formal photograph of the Choir, c.1884. Photograph: Rowe Library.

From the 1920s onwards much around the Chapel was adorned and beautified. The Choir was put into cassocks, and, albeit reluctantly, Mann yielded to encouragements to widen the repertoire to include Tudor music. He also accepted, though with somewhat less alacrity, the growing influence of incunable technology. A radio broadcast of a Sunday service was made on 4 May 1926, although whether the old 'meat-safe' microphone, on its special trolley, could give a faithful representation of the Chapel's acoustic was another matter. On 30 May 1927 the new HMV mobile van visited Cambridge, recording in both King's and St John's. Mann was dissatisfied with the result, it is said, and refused to allow any of the recordings to be released, and so St John's College Choir entered the record catalogues before King's! In 1928 the

Christmas Eve service was broadcast for the first time. During the previous two years the unwieldy Round-Sykes microphones had been superseded by early Marconi-Reisz types, which could be slung on cables in the Chapel as well as put on more conventional stands, making such a broadcasting exercise far easier, and more acceptable to both congregation and choir. By the following year, when Mann died, having served the College for 53 years, the Choir and its activities took a form which would be recognisable today.

The past 68 years, since Mann's death, have seen the King's College Choir consolidate and expand its role. Under Boris Ord and Milner-White in the 1930s the establishment enjoyed something of a 'golden era'. The Choir's main duty was then, as now, the singing of the term-time services in the Chapel, but Boris could exploit his academic connections to enlarge the repertoire, with immediate effect, beyond all recognition. In Mann's time the Choir had directed itself, since he regarded it as the Organist's duty to do all the organ playing necessary. Occasionally, when the anthem was unaccompanied, he would go down and join the basses at the end of the back row, nodding across, as he sang, to indicate the beat. Despite increasing age Mann retained a rich bass voice. In 1932 conducting desks were added to the west ends of the boys' stalls, and it was from these that Boris Ord and David Willcocks, his successor from 1958, would direct the Choir, using nothing more than an unobtrusive, single finger upon the desk.

New opportunities arose. The year after the founding, in 1935, of the British Council for Relations with Other Countries the Choir was invited to tour Holland, Germany, Denmark and Sweden—the first time it had performed outside the country. Concert-recitals were given, such as one of Tudor church music, as part of the 1933 Cambridge Festival of English Music, held when the Incorporated Society of Musicologists, under Dent's ægis, had their conference in Cambridge. Interestingly enough, this type of programme had first been heard with the combined choirs of King's, Trinity and St John's back in 1923, the year of festivities to celebrate the 350th anniversary of the birth of Orlando Gibbons. In 1931 an Organ Studentship was founded in Dr. Mann's memory, obviating the need for an unofficial assistant organist, and thus making the Choir's educational function complete.

From the beginning of the Empire Service of the BBC in December 1932 the *Festival of Nine Lessons and Carols* was heard abroad. For some curious and perhaps technical reason, which cannot now be determined, the BBC did not take the service in 1930, broadcasting a concert instead. Initially only a part of the service could be heard simultaneously abroad, and it was not until better steel-tape equipment could replace the unreliable Blattnerphones at Maida Vale, in June 1935, that the 30-minute portions of it could be time-delayed for retransmission round the globe. In 1938 the carol service was recorded in its entirety on Phillips-Miller sound-film, and this copy was almost worn out making dubbings to circulate for re-broadcast to the troops for morale-boosting purposes during World War II. Perhaps the making of a considerably higher-fidelity recording was to compensate for the BBC National programme that year preferring to broadcast the Test Match from South Africa on Christmas Eve, leaving it to the Regional programmes to take the carols. This led to the absurdity that King's could be heard in Australia and North America, but not in the western region of England nor in Northern Ireland. It was the last time that anything of this sort occurred.

During the early 1940s many choral scholars and the organ scholar (David Willcocks), as well as Boris Ord himself, joined up with the armed forces, and Harold Darke acted as Organist. Although the Choir School continued to function, the lower voices were provided by a very few choral scholars, before their inevitable call-up, and a number of volunteers with university connections. Nevertheless, the Choir continued to broadcast, and, for the first time, a number of Evensongs were taken. Previously services other than Christmas Eve had come only from St Paul's Cathedral or Westminster Abbey in London, but with the onslaught of bombing raids it was decided to make the broadcasts from places of

greater safety, although the policy was always to regard the venue as anonymous until after the transmission. The Choir also contributed to a film, made by the GPO Film Unit, entitled *Christmas Under Fire*. One object of this film was to bring home to those across the Atlantic the plight of Britain at that time, in the hope of encouraging help in the hostilities. The college authorities acceded to the request for this filming, in 1941, in case it might also turn out to be the last. Throughout this period the Chapel was devoid of its glass, stored, it was rumoured, deep in some Welsh slate mine, although in fact mostly in the cellars of the Gibbs building. In its place was blackout material, and grey tar-paper to let in a little light, while it rattled furiously in the wind.

Soon after resumption of 'normal services' after the war the Choir made its first commercial carol record. There had been no gramophone recording since a second, abortive, visit by the mobile van in 1929, although without 'Daddy' Mann to forbid it, two recordings from 1927 were eventually released in 1930 on a single disc. The increase in broadcasting, initially as part of a choral 'war effort', now remained as a habit, and, in the immediate post-war years, before the regular BBC Choral Evensong series from around the country had become established, King's made frequent programmes, as often as every week for a month. Under Boris Ord there were 78rpm gramophone records of English church music, contributing to an anthology, master-minded by E.H. Fellowes, and which included other choirs. These were recorded from 1949 to 1952. The Choir also toured Belgium and Holland in 1949, and Switzerland in 1952 and 1955. In 1954 television arrived, a shortened version of the Christmas Eve service being performed to TV cameras and then recorded on to film, as was the only technique available in the days before magnetic video recording. TV broadcasting did not take place again until 1963, and it has never been the same regular fixture as the Christmas Eve service has been for a radio audience.

With the advent of magnetic tape and the long-playing record the scope for choir recordings widened, although carols remained an assured commercial success, and therefore of continuing appeal to any record company. In fact, from the earliest electric recordings in England in 1926, hymns and carols have represented the two church-choir commodities most beloved of the manufacturers. In 1954, through a fruitful association with the fledgling independent company, Argo Records, LPs were made by Boris and the Choir, one of the most enduring being the first of a planned series of choral music by Orlando Gibbons. Further concerts were given with orchestra, some of them broadcast, and the mainstays of this programming were the Schütz *Christmas Story*, the Brahms *Alto Rhapsody* and Fauré's *Requiem*.

In 1957, his health having been failing for a few years, Boris Ord began the process of handing over the reins to his former organ scholar, David Willcocks. As has been mentioned, Willcocks' undergraduate career had been interrupted by war service, during which he had been awarded the Military Cross, and after a brief time as a Fellow of King's he had held the post of Organist at Salisbury Cathedral and then at Worcester. For a year he acted as Assistant Organist to Boris Ord, and assumed charge in 1958.

During the period of almost forty years since David Willcocks took charge in the chapel the King's College Choir has reached an increasing audience, through recordings, broadcasts and foreign tours. The first visit outside Europe was a trip to Ghana, Sierra Leone and Nigeria in 1972. It was particularly requested that the Choir should perform some of its Christmas repertoire, but it seemed strange to

7   The Choir processing from the Senate House after the Memorial Service for Queen Victoria in 1901. Photograph: Rowe Library.

8   A dinner party given in a choral scholar's room in 1927 to celebrate Arthur Mann's Golden Jubilee. Photograph: Rowe Library.

9   A gathering of choral scholars to celebrate Boris Ord's Silver Jubilee in 1955. Photograph: Rowe Library.

sing of the 'winter's snow' and a 'cold, cold winter's night' in a land where such phenomena were totally unknown. The following year the Choir made its trans-atlantic debut. While, for English choirs generally, climbing on to a plane to make visits round the world has become commonplace, and, last summer, the Choir was able to make its first tour to South Africa, the principal function of the King's College Choir has been, and always will remain, the provision of music of the highest standard to adorn the worship in the Chapel. The boys are, in many re-spects, ordinary schoolboys, although the experience of being a chorister at King's, as at many other full-time choral establishments, is something which makes those years special. Many choristers have gone on to musical careers, but, equally, others have developed in totally different spheres. For the choral scholars, all read for a university degree, and the academic standard of the Choir these days is high. There is nothing of a 'back-door' entry to Cambridge through being accepted as a choral scholar, and, while the work in the Choir is undoubtedly hard, the time necessary to devote to normal undergraduate studies is no less. But none can forget his own time as a member of this Choir. As Sir David Willcocks has re-marked, 'Each of us thinks that the Choir was best in his own particular era'. Yet the maintaining of the standard today is as important as it has been at any time during the past 120 years, and all have been proud to have been a small part of a great tradition which has now spanned five and a half centuries.

© Andrew Parker, 1997

## Organists and Directors of Music of King's College in the 20th Century

10   Arthur Mann
1876–1929
Photograph: Patrick Robertson

11   Boris Ord
1929–1957
Photograph: Maurice Hill

12   Harold Darke*
1941–1945
Photograph: Hubert Darke

13   David Willcocks
1957–1973
Photograph: College Library

14   Philip Ledger
1974–1982
Photograph: Nigel Luckhurst

15   Stephen Cleobury
1982–
Photograph: Nigel Luckhurst

* Harold Darke was Acting Organist during Boris Ord's absence on war service.

*Chapter Two*

# MICHAELMAS TERM

16

## The Statue of Henry VI on Provost Hacumblen's Lectern
*George Pattison, Dean of King's College*

The lectern, topped by the figurehead-like statue of Henry VI, epito-mises the fusion of piety and publicity that has characterised the Chapel from its earliest days. As a memorial of the Founder, it recalls both his private devotion and his royal power. It is richly decorated with the same symbolic royal roses that adorn the Chapel throughout, but it is also engraved with exquisite images of the four evangelists and their sym-bolic animals—John and his eagle, Matthew and his angel, Luke and his ox, and Mark and his lion (images taken from the vision of Ezekiel, chap-ter one). This reminds us that although Henry is to be honoured as Founder of the College, the true foundation of the worship offered in the Chapel is scripture—and above all, the gospels. This is not merely a theological point, for scripture provides the framework and source of the daily serv-ices and, of course, it is the nine lessons from scripture that shape the *Festival of Nine Lessons and Carols*.

**17** King Henry VI as
portrayed on Provost
Hacumblen's Lectern.
Photograph: Penny Cleobury.

# The Headmaster of King's College School

*Gerald Peacocke, Headmaster 1977-93*

King Henry VI's plans for the Choir of the 'College roial of Our Lady and Seynt Nicholas' at Cambridge stipulated that the College should be responsible for the education and welfare of the 16 choristers under the supervision of a Master over the Choristers. This person was for centuries commonly a College servant—at one point even the Clare College baker! Nevertheless, the choristers' education must have been taken seriously, for in the 16th and 17th centuries the boys' educational accommodation, a room within the College, was known as the King's College Grammar School. It cannot, however, be claimed that the schooling was truly professional until the great reform and the opening of the new King's College School in West Road in 1876. That event meant that the Master over the Choristers was henceforth to hold the further title of Headmaster, a man who was a qualified teacher rather than a College servant.

The new Head faces the opening of his first year in September. All is ready, and all are prepared to welcome the choristers and other boarders. He greets these boys, many of the new ones greatly excited, some masking—like himself?—their nervousness and apprehension with bravado. He becomes acquainted with their parents. Already that night he goes to bed more confidently: the process of familiarisation has begun. Next morning he meets the array of new and current day boys and girls, including the little pre-preppers, and many of their parents. Now follows his first experience of the Chapel: he joins the entire school as it crocodiles across the Backs into the great edifice for the term's opening service. He will have the enchanting experience of observing the astonished and awe-struck faces of the children when they enter the noble space for the first time, and even of catching an exclamation or two. On one such occasion I overheard a little boy simply say, 'Blimey!'.

As he shepherds and accompanies the boys in their routines and on special occasions throughout the year, the Master over the Choristers increasingly picks up and learns to respect the special features of the choristers' lives. Amongst these are the sheer professional discipline of what they do in the Choir; and the range of music that they learn and sing. Sometimes a boy's voice will break early and he will have a final, specially chosen service to sing. When I asked one such 'pensioner' how he felt shortly after he had sung his last service, he replied: 'It's all this time I have, Sir—it's weird!'.

The Head and his staff have to learn another crucial aspect of these busy boys' lives, the opportunity to relax and revert to playful childhood after the strict concentration of their obligations as singers. Both the boys and we have to learn how to deal with this, how to achieve a balance between the Choir's and the individual's needs.

The Master over the Choristers can share in most or all of the special events that enliven the chorister's year. There are the College Feasts where the boys can enjoy sumptuous food in the Great Hall in return for singing for their supper, a grace and some glees to the assembled guests—a neat reversal of the practice of earlier centuries when the boys repaid the College's munificence by serving its members at table. There are beautiful services to appreciate: the dignified Requiems of All Souls' Day and Remembrance Sunday; the wondrous eastward flow from darkness to light of the Advent Carol Service; the services in memory of King Henry VI, on Founder's Day (6 December) and Founder's Obit (21 May) [commemorating the King's death] with the ceremony of presenting white lilies and roses at the altar, the emblems of Eton and King's. Most special of all, both to the choristers and the Headmaster, are the Christmas and Easter services.

Over the period preceding Christmas, the choristers enjoy their 'Choir Time', when the school term is over and only the choristers and senior probationers are in residence. Between CD and TV recordings they can relax with cooking, cracker-making, a little drama or concert, outings to the pantomime with Mr. Cleobury, parties and games. One such party is given by the Headmaster and his wife, another is the visit to the Vice-Provost in College, when the choristers receive food and drink, each his own chosen recorded or printed music, and a silver Churchill crown, their presents from the College. They will also have a little time at home or with friends before returning for the climax of the King's year, the *Festival of Nine Lessons and Carols* on Christmas Eve. What a privilege for the Headmaster to participate in this wonderful occasion, the College's gift to the City of Cambridge. After the service and tea in College, a family party follows in the School, the choristers prepare for Christmas Day and are tucked up in bed. For me that was always a short night, for my most important task awaited me in the morning: the distribution of the choristers' stockings. A pact allowed the boys to prepare booby traps—dry, not wet!—pillows, duvets and harmless squirting devices to greet the arrival of the Headmaster. In return I would dress up, leave the big sack of stockings in the corner and try to outflank and surprise the boys. Once in the appointed dormitory I would briefly be assaulted with the pillows and traps. When I yelled 'Pax!' the assault would stop, we wished each other a happy Christmas, I distributed their stockings, and we would get ready for breakfast—with more presents. The joyful Sung Eucharist, with brass band welcoming the vast congregation, a Mozart Mass and some carols, rounds off the services, and so the choristers and their families, and the Headmaster and his staff go home to start their own festivities.

It is a pleasure for the Headmaster to be on hand and on duty throughout Christmas, Easter and Summer periods of Choir Time. The Easter services are the loveliest of all. The warmer weather allows excursions and punting on the river. The Summer term brings the excitements of May Week, with its noisy balls and the College's May Week Concert. The worries of scholarship and Common Entrance exams are now over. The June break (a two-week holiday) is most welcome. When the choristers return in July, those soon to leave enjoy a special programme of events organised by the Deputy Head.

Finally, there are the Choir's commitments outside the Chapel: concerts in Cambridge and elsewhere in the UK; tours overseas to all parts of the globe. Such tours are a time when the Headmaster, if he is fortunate enough to accompany them, gets to know the choral scholars better and is fully involved with the choristers in their travel, rehearsals, concerts, services and other public engagements. If they are not staying with hosts, he will also help look after them in their hotels or hostels. Tours offer a wonderful experience of the world to all participants, and for the Master over the Choristers, a further insight into these boys, their characters, needs, obligations, their capacity for professional performance at so high a level, and for sheer enjoyment. With all the year's tests and experiences behind and those of further years ahead of him, the man fortunate enough to be Headmaster of King's knows that King Henry's miraculous Choir and Chapel form the rock upon which he securely stands.

## The Mann Organ Scholar at King's

*James Vivian, o.s. 1993-7*

The Christmas Eve Carol Service is the most famous event in the Choir's calendar. This act of worship displays the major duty of the King's organ scholar to millions of people, namely, to provide organ voluntaries and accompaniments to the Choir. However, not all of the responsibilities are as glamorous (or as nerve-racking!) as this. Many hours during the day and night are spent in the organ loft, meticulously preparing music for the services. Frequently, anybody walking through Front Court late at night will be serenaded by the loud strains of the Chapel

**19** Montage: The choristers lead a normal school life. Photographs: King's College School.

organ. Time must also be devoted to the University's Tripos (exams): the scholarship is effectively a full-time job, so careful selection must be made when choosing lectures.

The day will often begin at 8.15am with a chorister practice that involves getting up much earlier than most fellow undergraduates. In addition, the organ scholar will sometimes be responsible for the choral scholars when the Director of Music is away. It is therefore important that he gains the respect of both the boys and his choral scholar contemporaries—a distinction must be made between under-graduate fun and the professionalism that the Chapel demands! A strange dichotomy exists—on one hand, he is a member of a team that is answerable to the Director of Music, but on other occasions he is required to take on the leader's role.

The organ scholar must also learn to be flexible in all situations. This is particularly the case when the Choir performs concerts in strange venues: practice time on these instruments (some of which may not have pipes or are virtually unplayable!) is limited. Therefore, the organ scholar is often separated from the rest of the choir so that his practice time is maximised. However, the rewards of the job make the scholarship more than tenable. The Chapel organ is perhaps the finest accompanying instrument of its type and the experience gained from the various activities make the scholarship invaluable.

**20** The present organ scholars, James Vivian (seated) and Robert Quinney in the organ loft. Photograph: Penny Cleobury.

# The Choral Scholar Conductors (the 'beaters')
*Keith Roberts, c.s. 1991-4*

To the first-time visitor to a choral service at King's, the sight of two choral scholars beating time for a large proportion of the service while the conductor appears to be taking a break in the organ loft may seem a little bizarre. Of course, there is an explanation. The reason is that it is easier for the 'beaters' to co-ordinate the intricacies of the psalmody [the art of singing psalms] besides giving the con-ductor a chance to listen (and watch) the Choir from a distance 'live'.

As the Choir embarks on a journey through the day's psalm, the beater steers it through with almost complete musical and story-telling control (while at the edge of thought is the nagging fear that one mistake—made all the more likely by having to beat and sing at the same time—might send the Choir crashing off the rails). In one of the old war-horses like Psalm 78, with unison fortissimo quad-ruple chants, tales of plagues and thunderbolts, the feeling is quite exhilarating. Personally, it ranks with the excitement and terror of the first carol service and Sunday evensongs in June as particularly uplifting experiences, especially trying to get the extra ounce of drama (not that the Choir usually needs prompting) with a tasteless ritenuto or accelerando while the Director of Music or organ scholar squirms upstairs. This may be one reason why beaters are rarely let loose on the rest of the service ...

In rehearsal, the beaters have an extra responsibility whenever the choir director wants the lateral view. This manifests itself in a trick that the beater likes to inflict to scare the choir into watching the beat. It will consist of an exaggerated up-beat which is left hanging in the air without the down-beat. Beware a singer who never watches; he will carry on singing, and because everyone else is supposed to have stopped, the resultant solo echoes accusingly around the building. This rarely catches the intended target (usually a chorister in a particularly dozy mood), who has the excellent self-defence mechanism of never coming in until he hears everyone else anyway! Instead it will catch out the conscientious chorister or choral scholar in a rare lapse, or the other beater, and it is very embarrassing for all concerned. On more than one occasion, the whole Choir has carried on regardless. However, having been the victim himself on many occasions in the past, the beater will always want revenge, so this tradition lingers on.

Therefore, while the tradition of beating seems an innocent enough way of making the conductor's life easier, it does in fact turn the most mild-mannered of choral scholars into dictators!

**21** Collegium Regale—the choral scholars of King's College Choir. Photograph: Benjamin Finn.

**22 & 23** A potential chorister and choral scholar are auditioned for places in the Choir. Photographs: Penny Cleobury.

# An Introduction to Collegium Regale
## (the choral scholars of King's College Choir)

*Jonathan Rippon, c.s. 1992-5*

When King Henry VI founded King's College in the 15th century, he established a choir consisting of 16 boy choristers and six lay clerks to sing the services in the Chapel. The last lay clerk left in 1927, and nowadays the 14 members of the alto, tenor and bass sections are choral scholars who study as undergraduates of King's College. They remain in the Choir for a maximum three years, reading many different subjects for their degrees.

The choral scholars have their own singing group, independent of the Choir, called 'Collegium Regale' (the Latin for 'Royal College'). They perform a wide variety of unaccompanied music, specialising in 16th-century English ecclesiastical repertoire and arrangements in close harmony of pop songs, made by present and former choral scholars. Throughout the year 'Coll Reg' provides entertainment at dinners, private functions, business conferences or parties, mainly in Cambridge. They also raise money through regular charity concerts.

Many successful singing groups such as 'The King's Singers', 'The Light Blues' and 'The Scholars' have sprung from these roots. The membership changes every year, giving the group a fresh image and new ideas. In the Michaelmas term, the Musical Director of the group (one of the choral scholars) trains them and steadily builds up the repertoire for that year. Annually they make a concert tour in two groups of seven of the North and South of England respectively. In 1994 'Coll Reg' represented the College touring America. In 1995 the group recorded its first CD, entitled 'Collegium Regale: Unplugged' and in 1996 travelled to Japan.

## Remembrance Sunday

This is commemorated on the Sunday nearest to 11 November, and is marked in the Chapel at 6pm, when the Requiem Mass by either Fauré or Duruflé is sung liturgically. At the morning service in Chapel a short anthem, *For the Fallen*, is performed. It was written by Douglas Guest who was the second King's organ scholar, being up at King's from 1935-9. He became Director of Music at Uppingham in 1945 and successively the Organist of Salisbury and Worcester Cathedrals and Westminster Abbey.

He served with great distinction during the War, but sadly lost many of the friends who had been up at Cambridge with him. The deep sorrow at the loss of these friends and so many of Britain's youth crystallised in the composition of this anthem with words by Lawrence Binyon. *For the Fallen* was composed for the Remembrance Day service at Westminster Abbey in 1971.

24   The anthem *For the Fallen* was composed especially for Remembrance Sunday by Douglas Guest. Photograph: Penny Cleobury.

## Advent Sunday

In the service for Advent Sunday, the procession moves from the west to the east end of the Chapel. The liturgy symbolises the progression from darkness, which precedes the story of Creation in Genesis, to the light of the vision of the City of God.

**25** David Willcocks and the Choir processing, interspersed with candle-bearers, during the Advent Carol Service. Photograph: Unknown.

## The Advent Carol Service 1992 (our first!)

*Simon Eadon, chorister parent*

Darkness and silence, that is how it starts, just flickering candles casting a warm glow on the congregation. We can just see the Choir appearing at the west end of the Chapel through the organ screen arch. The music, by Francis Grier, is loud and stirring. Although we cannot see the Choir's progress up the aisle, we are aware of the volume of the music becoming more intense as they near the screen. This is reinforced by the growing light in the Chapel: as each window is passed by the Choir, so it is lit up. The visual and aural senses are aware of the imminent appearance of the Choir—plotting its movement up the aisle with laser precision—even though the focus of our attention cannot be seen directly. This is Advent. The Choir becomes visible and eventually reaches the altar, but not before Cantoris and Decani have respectively gone into a North and South side-chapel to sing a carol. The singing, even under this adverse condition, is impeccable. Our lasting impression of this service must be the drama of it: darkness to light, silence to glass-shattering harmony. Fantastic!

**26** The crowded Chapel viewed through a rope-hole in the roof at the Advent Carol Service of 1959. Photograph: Rowe Library.

**27**  Her Majesty the Queen and Prince Philip with the Provost attending the Advent Carol Service in 1991. Photograph: *Cambridge Evening News.*

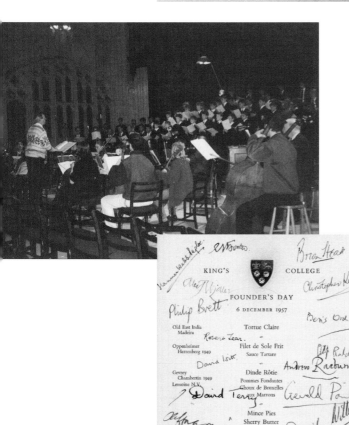

**28**  A rehearsal in the Chapel, for the Founder's Day concert when former choral scholars rejoin the Choir. Photograph: Penny Cleobury. Below: Founder's Day Feast Menu.

# From 'Sylvia Plath's Letters Home'

Last Sunday, before the deluge of this week, I shared the most magnificent experience with him: Advent service at the King's Chapel. Since Mallory belongs to King's College, he got two tickets. Honestly, mother, I never have been so moved in my life. It was evening, and the tall chapel, with its cobweb lace of fan-vaulting, was lit with myriads of flickering candles, which made fantastic shadows play on the walls, carved with crowns and roses. The King's Choir boys processed down through the chapel singing in that clear bell-like way children have: utterly pure and crystal notes.

I remembered all the lovely Christmas times we've had as a family, caroling with our dear friends, and the tears just streamed down my face in a kind of poignant joy. The organ pealed out and the hymn was that magnificent one *Wachet Auf (Now Let Every Tongue Adore Thee)* which was so beautifully familiar...

*ed. Aurelia Schober Plath, Harper and Row, New York, 1975.*

# Founder's Day

The Founder's Day (Henry VI's birthday) is 6 December. This is the day on which we remember St Nicholas, one of the saints to whom the Chapel is dedicated (the other being the Blessed Virgin Mary). Today, the College holds its celebrations at the weekend nearest to the date. These include a special Evensong, followed by a feast, on the Friday evening, and on the Saturday, an early evening concert (instead of Evensong), in which former choral scholars join with the Chapel Choir and School's Choir, followed by a dinner for these former students.

*Chapter Three*

# CHRISTMAS

30

## *The Adoration of the Magi* by **Rubens**
*George Pattison*

**29** (left)  *The Adoration of the Magi* painted by Peter Paul Rubens (1577-1640) which is mounted behind the high altar in the Chapel. Photograph: College Library.

When Rubens' painting of *The Adoration of the Magi* was installed behind the altar in 1968 it caused a storm of controversy. It is true that the installation involved changing the appearance of the whole of the east end and it is also true that its warm, sensuous colours strike a very different tone from that of the windows. Yet it is fitting that a Chapel devoted to Mary and associated the world over with Christmas should have such an image as its focal point. Indeed, it is in the winter months, when the great windows are steeped in shadow, that the flowing lines and glowing colours of the painting reveal themselves most alluringly, drawing us in to the mysteries of the incarnation and adoration. Sitting meditatively before this great work of art, visitors and worshippers from many cultures and many faiths find themselves becoming involved as pilgrims, like the wise men themselves, journeying towards the luminous centre of the painting, the infant Christ, who is light itself, Light of light and Giver of light to all walkers in darkness.

# How did the *Festival of Nine Lessons and Carols* start?
## *Penny Cleobury*

The story behind the service which has made King's College Chapel an international institution began in 1878. In that year the Rev. G.H.S. Walpole was appointed Succentor of Truro Cathedral in Cornwall. (At this time a small wooden building served as the cathedral, as the stone building was still under construction.) Walpole was concerned that many of the congregation for Midnight Mass on Christmas Eve had spent the evening celebrating in the local public houses, and consequently their thoughts were far removed from the true meaning of Christmas! To provide a more fitting prelude to the Christmas services, he organised a carol service to be sung by the cathedral choir starting at 10pm on the Eve.

However, he felt that the service was too similar to the form of morning and evening prayer. So, after Christmas, he approached his Bishop, Edward White Benson, for help with the form this service should take. Bishop Benson, together with his Precentor, Augustus Donaldson, delved back into medieval service books and drew up a service of carols interspersed with nine short lessons. The lessons were devised to range from innocence to wisdom and were read by officers of the church beginning with a chorister and ending with the Bishop. After the ninth lesson came an anthem from *Messiah*, the *Magnificat* and a final prayer.

In 1883 Bishop Benson became Archbishop of Canterbury and his carol service became more widely known. Just six weeks after the end of the First World War in December 1918, the then new Dean of King's, Eric Milner-White, introduced the service to King's Chapel for the first time. He devised a Bidding Prayer which many think has led this service to become one of the most loved in the world, capturing as it does the spirit of unity and peace 'as well as the joy and worship of us all at the coming of our Christ'.

**31** Eric Milner-White, Dean, 1918-34. Photograph: College Library.

The service began with the carol *Up! Good Christen Folk*, with *Once in Royal David's City* following it. But in 1919 the service was revised with the latter coming at the beginning, as it has done ever since. Milner-White also rearranged the lessons and replaced the traditional extracts from *Messiah* with carols. The popularity of the service grew and in 1928 the BBC broadcast it for the first time. With the exception of 1930 it has been broadcast ever since, even through the Second World War, when the name of the Chapel could not be mentioned for security reasons. Nowadays it is broadcast throughout the world and can reach an audience of many millions. For many people the service marks the beginning of Christmas.

## The BBC Christmas Broadcasts
### *James Whitbourn, BBC Producer*

Broadcasts of religious services broadly fall into two camps: the first comprises broadcasts of those services which are designed for liturgical use within a church or cathedral and upon which the BBC eavesdrops.

The second type comprises those occasions which are specifically planned for radio or television, even if they also have life as genuine church occasions. Several years of discussion between the College and the BBC have led us to the conclusion that, for the present, both approaches are to be used simultaneously in our broadcasts of carol services from King's.

So, on Christmas Eve, the BBC broadcasts the *Festival of Nine Lessons and Carols* live at 3pm. This is essentially a relay of the service conceived by the College, and falls into the eavesdropping category. But the Christmas shoppers in Cambridge

**32** Montage: Christmas at King's. Photographs: *Cambridge Evening News.*

will have noticed large BBC lorries in King's Parade a fortnight or so beforehand. These house the television equipment used to record a different (but similar) service which has been conceived from the outset with the needs of television in mind, and which therefore falls into the other category. There are not always nine lessons, and the lessons are not always the same. The music is chosen with a particular audience in mind. The lessons are read not from the huge lectern which dwarfs the readers, but from side stalls, where they are not hidden away from the cameras. There is a small amount of additional lighting in the Chapel—not enough to spoil the atmosphere of calm, but enough that any regular chapel-goer would notice the difference.

The television recording is broadcast either on Christmas Eve, or a day or two beforehand, and its time can be moved to fit in with other programmes in the schedule.

(James Whitbourn is a producer for BBC Religious Broadcasting. David Kremer and he are responsible for the broadcasts of *Carols from King's* and *A Festival of Nine Lessons and Carols*. The television Director is David Kremer and the Production Assistant is Gill Blunk.)

## 'Carols from King's' (the television programme)
### *James Whitbourn*

The two services (one for television and the other for radio) are planned together, and the preparation begins in January or February. This is a good time to reflect on the previous year's broadcasts, while they are still fresh in the mind. The BBC producers meet with the Dean and the Director of Music to discuss any points raised.

The general shape of the live Christmas Eve service is unchanging. The televised service, however, demands some early thought, and the first move is made by the Dean, who is responsible for choosing lessons and readings. There is time for discussion and consultation, and by the middle of the year the outline is in place. Over the summer, the Director of Music makes his musical choices for the television programme and at the same time will be thinking about his likely selections for the Christmas Eve service, for which some of the music will be the same.

Once the choices of readings and music have been made, progress falls next to the television director and production. Just as the musical director marks in phrasing and breathing bar by bar, so the television director decides on camera angles and lighting effects. As the musical director thinks of key sequences and tempi, so the television director considers the possibilities of movement and space in every frame. Every shot is planned and timed. Every shot is marked into the full musical

33  Boris Ord reading a lesson in the first televised carol programme in 1954. Photograph: The Cambridgeshire Collection.

**34** BBC television vans outside King's College. Photograph: Penny Cleobury.

score. Then the camera cards are made. These are rather like the instrumental parts given to individual members of an orchestra. Each camera operator has his own 'part', and will work from these cards for three days during rehearsals and recordings.

The tradition of televising services began in 1954, so by now the College is well used to the presence of the large Outside Broadcast unit which takes up residence around the middle of December.

Rigging equipment in King's College Chapel is an experience of mixed emotions. Here, on one hand, is one of the most imposing buildings in the world, and it is a privilege to work in a place of such breathtaking beauty. On the other hand, it was built many hundreds of years before radio and television were invented, and no thought was given by architects to the requirements of engineers who need to secure cables and cameras to the fabric of the chapel and suspend microphones from the vaults. It is slow work, because it must be done carefully.

By Friday evening, everything is ready, and the choir rehearsal begins. In fact, two rehearsals are happening simultaneously: while the Choir prepares its performance of all the music, the BBC crew prepares its performance of technical equipment. The equipment is mechanical, electrical, magnetic and optical, and there is plenty of room for technical failure. This is what rehearsal is for.

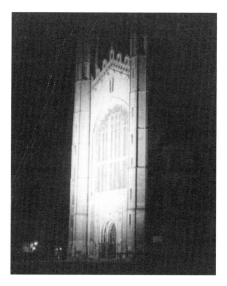

**35** The Chapel floodlit for the television recording. Photograph: Penny Cleobury.

Saturday sees a complete run-through of the service, and the day ends with a rehearsal and recording session with the readers. By recording the readings in advance, neither the camera nor the congregation disturb each other.

'Run VT', comes the command from the BBC control vehicle. On Sunday, the service is recorded for real. Once the first carol has begun, the floor manager retreats into the shadows and emerges only when the final chord of the voluntary has died away. The director, if you like, has composed the television script, but now lets the production assistant 'conduct' the work, while the vision mixer 'leads' the performance.

Seventy-five minutes later comes the welcome sound 'stop VT'. The videotape machine which records the programme is halted and everyone can breathe again. As the congregation leaves the Chapel, the Director of Music makes his way round to the control vehicle and settles down with the production team to review the entire programme. He and the producers make comments about the music and consider any possible improvements that might be made. There is not much scope for recording anything very differently now: there is only a short session in the evening for tidying small corners and to give the director a chance to record any close-ups he needs.

Walking down King's Parade at lunchtime the following day, one can see only a few remnants of the BBC still to be cleared away. It is said that there is nothing faster than a BBC de-rig!

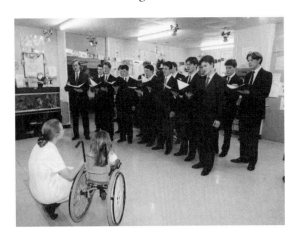

## 'King's—isn't that the place where the Carols come from?'

*Ian Moore, c.s. 1979-82*

Over the years, the *Festival of Nine Lessons and Carols* has become one of the most cherished symbols of Christ's Incarnation amidst this increasingly secular world. Its elements, deceptively simple, of biblical narration and musical illumination have, and will always, cast an hypnotic spell upon all alike.

Many spend more than a day queueing outside the College gates for this event. Why? On a facile level we can see that, by doing so, they gain 'the best seats'—much like the Proms or January sales—but is there any more to this rather eccentric, essentially English, phenomenon? Why has this sequence of oft-repeated readings and brief pieces of music become such an important part of our celebration of Christmas?

I have been found outside King's every Christmas for many years, even before becoming a member of the Choir for three years. And here I must confess great difficulty in describing what is, for me, an intensely contemplative, deeply personal time. My solitary vigil outside King's—invariably three days and nights before Christmas Eve—is spent contemplating the mystery of the Incarnation. Each year, through music and poetry I enter into my own pilgrimage to the manger. Over the past twenty years I have developed more than adequate resources for warmth and comfort, yet I smile inwardly, avoiding explanation, as yet another passer-by asks me 'Why?'. I know that, through this discomforted, meditative discipline, my three day Advent, I too am able 'in heart and mind, to go even unto Bethlehem', and share in a small way the wondrous journey of the Magi.

**36** (top left)   Collegium Regale sing carols around Cambridge's Addenbrooke's Hospital in December. Photograph: *Cambridge Evening News.*

**37** (top right)   As a part of the Christmas celebrations, Collegium Regale sing carols in the yard of the *Eagle*, a nearby pub. Photograph: Peter Hill.

**38** (bottom left)   The Choir sings in Christmas concerts in London, often in the Barbican, the Royal Festival or Royal Albert Halls. Here, they performed with the Philharmonia orchestra and chorus in the Royal Albert Hall. Photograph: Penny Cleobury.

**39** (bottom right)   The Director of Music takes the choristers to the Pantomime— and recently the choral scholars have attended as well! Photograph: Jonathan Rippon.

**40** (right)   Jean Churchman, Deputy Head Porter brings a warm drink to Ian Moore, the first person in the queue for the Christmas Eve Carol Service. Photograph: *Cambridge Evening News.*

On the third day and sometimes, in milder years, earlier, on the second day, the queue begins to lengthen. Often it's a familiar group of friends who are prepared to queue overnight. In fact, some of us have known each other throughout the twenty years, meeting just this one time, in the queue, every year. Spontaneously, we enter into the marvellously spirited, vivacious time of the queueing: we sing, eat and drink together, share our joys, our sorrows, our unfulfilled dreams, glimpsing how our individual lives have changed, occasionally discussing the merits of the 'new' descants, commissioned composers, the changing face of Cambridge itself, but always sharing in the expectant joy of celebrating the first moments of Christmas together once more, as an extended family, when we are truly 'born this happy morning'.

Over the past ten years it has been revelatory to welcome more and more 'first-timers' from America, Australia, and the Far East. Exchanging anecdotes can go on through the increasingly cold night, encouraged by liberal doses of 'spiced' coffee. With our blankets, umbrellas and improvised shelters we move through to the even more inhospitably exposed west side of the Gibbs Building, at 6am, the time when doubts of our sanity rise in our foggy minds. Some find brief respite at this time for sleep, though at times we are forced to huddle together against the insidious cold and penetrating rain, the Scrooge-like 'conspirators' of winters in Cambridge.

Finally the Chapel doors are opened and, casting our sodden blankets and empty thermos flasks aside, we enter triumphantly and take those 'best seats' beside the Choir. And here, accompanied by those seasonal tunes on the organ, you will witness a most charming sight for, as the august members of King's and its sister College of Eton sweep past, to their allotted stalls, we furtively remove our shoes and, seduced by the blissfully comforting warmth of underfloor-heating, gently rest our heads on each other's shoulders and quietly fall into a deep slumber.

To this day I cannot hear Messiaen's *La Nativité* or Bach's *Von Himmel Hoch* variations without sinking into a slumber!

Now we are forcibly awakened to stand and honour the spectacle of a grand mayoral procession, glittering with chains-of-office, in honour of the one true leader who is to enter the Chapel as a child. But all is forgiven as those thousands within the impeccably filled Chapel, together with the millions of radio listeners, are swept up in that great exultant sequence, which needs no description here.

We leave, thoroughly enriched, though strangely bereft of words. We entered in light, depart in darkness, seemingly at odds with the message of Christmas, and somehow words can no longer contain the confusing cauldron of emotions; our spiritual elation, our inevitable parting, our thanksgiving for the Choir and Chapel, bathed in honeyed candlelight, this ephemeral Paradise. We beat a reluctant retreat into the temporal world, our train connections to Paddington, desperately hoping we will keep awake for our families when they drag us out to Midnight Mass!

(Ian has queued every year since 1976.)

## Christmas Eve at the Porter's Lodge
*Jean Churchman, Deputy Head Porter*

For anyone working in the Porter's Lodge, Christmas Eve is synonymous with the Carol Service. Every porter is on duty, usually from 10am to 5pm. For months we have answered telephone calls from all over the world, assuring people that yes, they do have to queue but there is every chance that they will get in, especially if they come early. We continually count and monitor the queue and point out to anyone over a certain number that there may not be much hope in waiting.

Days beforehand the great front lawn will have been roped off, and bins for rubbish line the route of the queue on the left hand side of the front court. Ian Moore and about a dozen others who have slept out on the cobbles the night before are let in to form the beginning of the queue on the far side of the Gibbs Building. The night porters allow them in from 6am, most of them trundle their seats and sleeping bags round and settle down to sleep again.

After that people arrive in droves; by 9am the queue has straggled round the court. The first job of the porters is to start moving it and getting people to camp closer together, moving deckchairs, umbrellas, food and blankets. This is always done with banter, chat and questions answered, usually assuring them that their belongings will be guarded by a porter when everything is finally stored under the great Jumbo Arch of the Gibbs Building.

**41** The Headmaster gives a party for the choristers just before Christmas. Photograph: Penny Cleobury.

During this hubbub of monitoring the queue, the choral scholars move down the outside of it singing carols. A porter moves in and out of the crowd with a black plastic bag, gathering rubbish. Quietly the police in the background check the Chapel and the immediate area.

In the Porter's Lodge the telephone rings continually, usually it is people asking if there is still any chance of getting in. The Head Porter, in his pinstriped trousers and tail jacket, has dusted off his top hat and uncapped the silver topped mace ready for his ceremonial walk. This mace is engraved with the

**42** Each Christmas the Director of Music gives the choral scholars a party, at which they present him with a toy. This tradition began in Boris Ord's time and the collection of toys is now extensive. Photograph: Jonathan Rippon.

**43** After the morning's rehearsal in Chapel, Collegium Regale sing carols to the people waiting in the queue. Photograph: James Hossack.

date 1695. Previously his job might have been done by the college barber, groom, scullery man or superintendent of works. It was only in 1861 that the position of Head Porter came into existence, our present Head Porter being ninth in line.

From 1pm, porters have gone to each section of the queue, encouraging people to stow their belongings under the Gibbs Arch. This is helped along by another porter or custodian who will stand guard in there during the service. We tell everyone that, once the queue starts to move, it will go into the Chapel very quickly, which is true. By 1.30pm the North doors are open, and at a given signal the porters allow the queue forward in batches. Once people are seated most porters return to the Lodge and wait for the choral scholars, who every year come to the Lodge and sing to us. This always has people gathering at the window of the Lodge, listening in delight and disbelief.

The Head Porter, now carrying mace and top hat, waits under the Lodge arch to greet the Provost and his wife, the Mayor, Sergeant-at-Mace and civic dignitaries. This group he conducts at a sedate pace to the Chapel with full ceremony. There's part relief that it's now in the hands of the Chapel staff and the Choir, but it always seems so busy. Fielding questions about the College generally, and the service on Christmas Day, the work of the porters goes on, and, until the people have actually attended the service and leave the grounds, we're all on duty. It's a great day—busy, but not arduous, and we all love being part of it.

# The BBC Christmas Radio Broadcast

*James Whitbourn*

Christmas, it is said, begins at 3pm on Christmas Eve. All the world over, people tune their radios to hear *A Festival of Nine Lessons and Carols* from the chapel of King's College, Cambridge, broadcast live by the BBC. The image has a certain romance in it: people in India, Africa, America and Australia, joining the congregation in the chapel, and millions of listeners in Britain. The broadcast is surely the most significant Christmas tradition of the twentieth century. With the help of the BBC, the gift has been extended to the nation and to the world, and they have taken it as their own. So in a period of three score and ten, it has become public property and a national asset.

44   The aerial erected by the BBC to transmit the *Festival of Nine Lessons and Carols* on the World Service. Photograph: Penny Cleobury.

The BBC van arrives at the College at about the same time as those at the head of the queue stake out their places. Two days before the Christmas Eve service is broadcast, the first load of equipment draws up outside the North door of the Chapel. The giant World Service aerial, which briefly dominates the Cambridge skyline on Christmas Eve, is parked at the front of the College.

The feel of the radio transmission is quite different from the television recording. By broadcasting the service live, the BBC effectively opens the doors of the Chapel to tens—perhaps hundreds—of millions of other people. It is relayed all over the world, with large areas now covered with high quality signals.

Most musicians will tell you that they enjoy the disciplines of live broadcasting, and the same applies to producers. Because there are no re-takes, more time is put into the preparation to ensure that everything is 'just so'.

The first thing, as with the television recording, is to get all the equipment in place. The King's Festival is the biggest church broadcast of the year. Because the broadcast is so important to so many people, the engineers like to take no chances, and the microphones are doubled up in case of an unexpected fault.

Next day is a day of preparation with the Choir. The musicians have already learnt all the music in their own rehearsals, and the Director of Music can judge the effect in the Chapel better than any of us. But the presence of microphones adds another dimension. Imagine the parallel between the set designer and lighting director in a theatre. The set designer can have a colour scheme perfectly worked out, but the lighting director can change it all at the touch of a button. So too with sound. A sound engineer can favour distant reverberation or the very close spot microphones, and time and care are taken in achieving a good balance.

The readers will already have been coached by the College Chaplain, but they appreciate the chance to rehearse in front of the microphones, and this is done on the morning of Christmas Eve. Later, the Choir will come in again for their final rehearsal.

Come 3 o'clock, the red light flashes and the Director of Music knows they are soon to be live on air. A row of choristers fix their eyes on him, wondering who will be chosen to begin the service with that famous solo verse. Back in London, the announcer begins in measured tones 'and now we go direct to the Chapel of King's College, Cambridge...' There, the Director of Music points to a chorister, beckons him forward and waits. Everyone else holds their breath. The red light comes on, and we are on air. 'Once in royal David's city', begins the choirboy. Christmas has come again.

# Writing the Commissioned Carol

## *John Rutter, composer of the Commissioned Carol for 1987*

Generally I find composition easiest when I know the performers, and preferably the occasion, that I am writing for. On both counts I was off to a good start when Stephen Cleobury telephoned me in 1987 with an invitation to write a carol for the *Festival of Nine Lessons and Carols.* The sound of King's College Choir and the acoustic of its Chapel have been part of my interior landscape ever since I was a Cambridge undergraduate in the 1960s; and, after all these many years, I am still moved and inspired by the Christmas Eve Festival, an event that seems to offer a ray of light and hope in a sometimes almost unbearably dark world. I said yes, and immediately started to search for a text, the essential first step in a vocal composition. I soon found what I was looking for in the works of Robert Herrick, whose simple, delightful verses have an intrinsically musical quality which has attracted many composers. His *Carroll for Newe Yeares Daye* summed up in three lines everything I wanted to express:

> What sweeter music can we bring
> Than a carol, for to sing
> The birth of this, our heavenly King?

Writing the music to these words took several hard, concentrated days. As always, one plays endlessly with intervals, melodic shapes, rhythms—the raw materials of music—until they feel right. That is to say, the music should *appear* to have sprung out of the words with no effort or contrivance, almost as if no one had composed it but it had, in some sense, always been there. As Stephen Sondheim memorably put it, 'What's hard is simple, what's natural comes hard'. But I do believe a carol *should* sound simple and natural, which may cost considerable effort on the part of the composer.

For me, a composition is finished when the deadline has arrived and there is no more time left to polish it, pick it to pieces, or rewrite it. On the appointed day, I delivered a manuscript to the King's Porter's Lodge, secure in the expectation that on Christmas Eve I would hear a performance as near perfection as any earthly musicians could achieve. I was not disappointed.

(A carol has been commissioned annually since 1983.)

# Christmas at King's (1992)

## *Ashley Grote, ch. 1991-5*

For me, Christmas started with the afternoon of 13 December. This was the afternoon when we made a BBC TV recording of *Carols from King's*. We form up in the ante-chapel, and a single boy sings *Once in Royal David's City*. We get as far as the stalls and because of a technical hitch, have to do it again. The service continues as per!

A couple of days see ice-skating, cracker-making, video-watching, a visit to the pantomime, parties in College and in the Headmaster's house. Then it's back to Chapel to record *Messiah*, three hours a day for approximately four days. After a home break, practices and rehearsals take up a couple more days until Christmas Eve: a balance test for the BBC, and the *Festival of Nine Lessons and Carols.* Three o'clock arrives, the chorister starts the solo first verse of *Once in Royal David's City*, and millions of people across the world are filled with joy. In the evening we relax with a family party at the School.

**45** The queue for the *Festival of Nine Lessons and Carols* on Christmas Eve morning. Photograph: Penny Cleobury.

After 'Santa' [the Headmaster] has called on the choristers next morning with our stockings amid a barrage of pillows and ingenious booby-traps, we visit Chapel finally for the Sung Eucharist with a Mozart Mass. A visit to the Vice-Provost, presents galore, lunch, and then home to enjoy the normal Christmas everyone else has.

What I will always remember are the couple of seconds of pure silence, when you look around the senior choristers, wondering who will be chosen to sing the solo verse. The red light flashes, the organ modulates to the opening notes, Mr. Cleobury smiles, beckons, the chosen boy steps forward, Mr. Cleobury gently conducts, and my first *Festival of Nine Lessons and Carols* has begun.

## The Original Bidding Prayer from
## A Festival of Nine Lessons and Carols

Beloved in Christ, be it this Christmas Eve our care and delight to prepare ourselves to hear again the message of the Angels, and in heart and mind to go even unto Bethlehem and see this thing which has come to pass, and the Babe lying in the manger.

Therefore let us read and mark in Holy Scripture the tale of the loving purposes of GOD from the first days of our sin unto the glorious Redemption brought us by this Holy Child: let us make this Chapel, dedicated to His pure and lowly Mother, glad with our carols of praise.

But first, because this of all things would rejoice His heart, let us pray to Him for the needs of the whole world, and all His people; for peace upon the earth He

46   After the Christmas Eve Service choristers enjoy a party with their families. Photograph: Simon Eadon.

47   The choral scholars and all the staff who helped with the service enjoy a dinner in the College hall followed by balloon games! Photograph: Penny Cleobury.

came to save; for love and unity within the one Church He did build; for brother-hood and goodwill amongst all men, and especially within the dominions of our sovereign lord King George, within this University and Town of Cambridge, and in the two royal and religious Foundations of King Henry VI here and at Eton.

And particularly at this time let us remember before Him the poor, the cold, the hungry, the oppressed; the sick and them that mourn; the lonely and the unloved; the aged and the little children; all those who know not the Lord Jesus, or who love Him not, or who by sin have grieved His heart of love.

Lastly let us remember before Him them who rejoice with us, but upon another shore and in a greater light, that multitude which no man can number, whose hope was in the Word made flesh, and with whom, in this Lord Jesus, we for evermore are one.

These prayers and praises let us humbly offer up to the Throne of Heaven, in the words which Christ himself hath taught us:

*Our Father, which art in heaven, Hallowed be thy Name. Thy kingdom come. Thy will be done, in earth as it is in heaven. Give us this day our daily bread. And forgive us our trespasses, As we forgive them that trespass against us. And lead us not into temptation; But deliver us from evil: For thine is the kingdom, the power, and the glory, For ever and ever. Amen.*

GOD, the Son of GOD, vouchsafe to bless and aid us; and unto the fellowship of the citizens above may the King of Angels bring us all. *Amen.*

**49** A chorister with Christmas gift. Photograph: Brian Head.

Complaint by phone.

MESSAGE

Quote!
Could you speed up your organ playing, its more like a dirge, & the speakers could be more human.

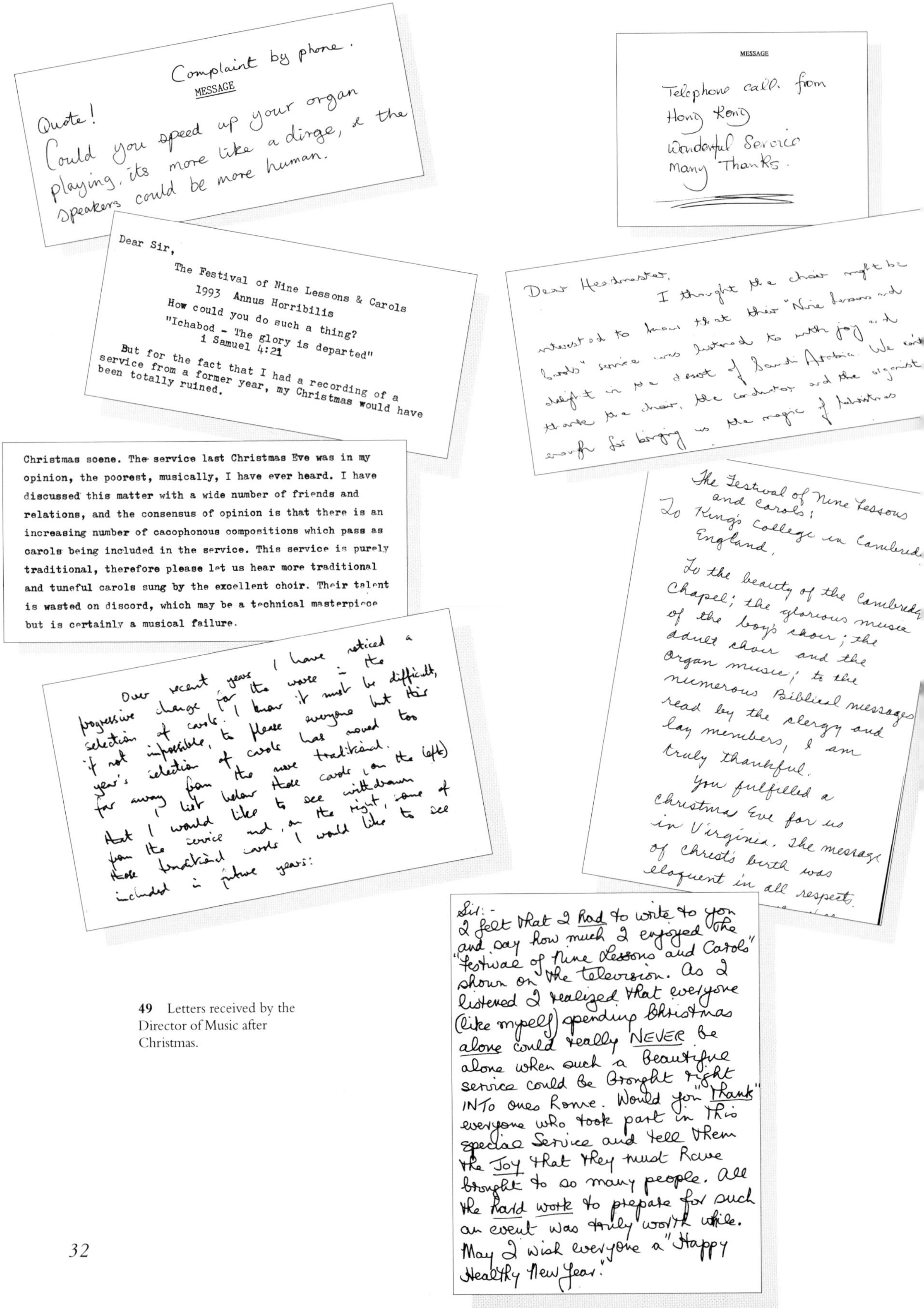

MESSAGE

Telephone call. from Hong Kong
Wonderful Service
Many Thanks.

Dear Sir,

The Festival of Nine Lessons & Carols
1993 Annus Horribilis
How could you do such a thing?
"Ichabod - The glory is departed"
1 Samuel 4:21

But for the fact that I had a recording of a service from a former year, my Christmas would have been totally ruined.

Dear Headmaster,
I thought the choir might be interested to know that their "Nine Lessons and Carols" service was listened to with joy and delight in the desert of Saudi Arabia. We can't thank the choir, the conductor and the organist enough for bringing us the magic of Christmas

Christmas scene. The service last Christmas Eve was in my opinion, the poorest, musically, I have ever heard. I have discussed this matter with a wide number of friends and relations, and the consensus of opinion is that there is an increasing number of cacophonous compositions which pass as carols being included in the service. This service is purely traditional, therefore please let us hear more traditional and tuneful carols sung by the excellent choir. Their talent is wasted on discord, which may be a technical masterpiece but is certainly a musical failure.

The Festival of Nine Lessons and Carols:
To King's College in Cambridge England,

To the beauty of the Cambridge Chapel; the glorious music of the boy's choir; the adult choir and the organ music; to the numerous Biblical messages read by the clergy and lay members, I am truly thankful.

You fulfilled a Christmas Eve for us in Virginia. The message of Christ's birth was eloquent in all respects.

Over recent years I have noticed a progressive change for the worse in the selection of carols. I know it must be difficult, if not impossible, to please everyone but this year's selection of carols has moved too far away from the more traditional. I list below those carols (on the left) that I would like to see withdrawn from the service and, on the right, some of those traditional carols I would like to see included in future years:

Sir:-
I felt that I had to write to you and say how much I enjoyed the "Festival of Nine Lessons and Carols" shown on the television. As I listened I realized that everyone (like myself) spending Christmas alone could really NEVER be alone when such a Beautiful service could be Brought right INTo ones home. Would you "Thank" everyone who took part in this special Service and tell them the JOY that they must have brought to so many people. All the hard work to prepare for such an event was truly worth while. May I wish everyone a "Happy Healthy New Year."

**49** Letters received by the Director of Music after Christmas.

# ENGLISH EDITION

*Watercolour of King's College Chapel painted by J.M.W. Turner 1796.*

# KING'S COLLEGE
# CAMBRIDGE

*W*elcome to King's, a college community whose members have been dedicated to education, religion, learning and research for over 550 years.

The young Henry VI laid the first stone of the King's College of Our Lady and St. Nicholas of Cambridge on Passion Sunday, 1441. King's was to have a provost and 70 poor scholars, drawn exclusively from Eton College, Henry's other foundation near Windsor. From the first, the College's buildings were intended to be a magnificent display of the power of royal patronage and Henry went to great lengths to ensure that King's College Chapel would be without equal in size and beauty.

Henry drew up detailed instructions for the construction of a 'great court' but only the Chapel was ever completed and even that took nearly a century. Despite its apparent unity of style, the Chapel is the product of three separate periods of construction; you can see the change in the external stone colouring (from white magnesian limestone to buff-coloured oolitic limestone) where building work was interrupted by the Wars of the Roses. Over the years, the original design was radically altered: for example, John Wastell, the master mason responsible for finishing the stonework of the building in 1515, discarded the plans for a conventional lierne vault and replaced it with the breathtaking fan vault - the largest in the world. The dark oak screen was a gift from Henry VIII, and bears his initials and those of Anne Boleyn, his queen. This dates it between 1533, when Henry married her, and 1536, when he had her executed. Another spectacular gift is the Adoration of the Magi which was painted by Rubens in 1634 for the Convent of the White Nuns at Louvain in Belgium. It stands behind the Altar, beneath the exquisite coloured glass of the great East Window.

The pattern of worship and significance of the Chapel in College life has changed over the centuries. Since 1918 the Chapel has been internationally

*Chapter Four*

# LENT TERM

50

## Lent
*George Pattison*

During the opening verse of *Once in Royal David's City* on Christmas Eve, I stand behind the Choir looking East, and what I see above the heads of Choir and congregation is the image of the crucifixion, etched in stark simplicity by the clear winter light. From Bethlehem—to Calvary, from the stable—to the cross: that is the story of the gospels, the story we travel in scripture and worship between Christmas and Holy Week, and the story that lies at the heart of their individual discipleship for many Christians. In a context which so powerfully evokes the beauty of holiness we need from time to time to look up and see the terrible cruel drama portrayed in the east windows—and portrayed with a power and a realism that leaves no hiding place for sentimentality. *This* is where it all leads to; *this* is the meaning of the sign that saves. In the background, scarcely visible to the unaided eye, the Good Centurion leans down from his horse and speaks to another soldier, 'Truly, this man was the son of God'. Can we look on such events and see in them an image of God's unconditional love, can we come to see that love in our own sufferings, can we become bearers of that love to others, no matter what the cost?

**51** (overleaf)    The central section of the Chapel's East window showing Christ crucified with the two thieves on either side. Photograph: College Library.

## Being a King's chorister…

*In 1836—Thomas Case (extracted from 'Memoir of a King's College chorister', written at the suggestion of A.H.Mann)*

In January … there was a notice that there would be a vacancy in the following March quarter and … many lads of the age of eight years were being coached up for the examination …from these were selected four (of whom I was one) for a future examination. What a time of musing it was by my Coach, who was one of the senior boys … I can remember his taking me several times to the 'backs' for a shouting stroll, viz., causing me to shout to him at lengthening distances, and if there were any crowds into which he could take me to shout, he embraced the opportunity of strengthening my voice, and, meanwhile, was practising me on the piano. There was so much Do, Re, Mi, that I wonder it did not make me very much quite a natural. The eventful day arrived for the trial of the four … Oh! the excitement as my dear mother mixed the yolk of an egg in a glass of sherry, which it was intended should make my voice mellow and strong, and probably as an anti-nervous draught!

I have said that eight of the senior boys had to 'wait' in the College Hall; the senior boy at the Senior Fellows' table on the boards or dais. The two next seniors were at the centre or Master of Arts' table … At the B.A. table were the next two boys, two at the Scholars', and one at the door to let the waiters in and out, and it was the duty of this boy to go to 'King's Spring' daily after Chapel and fetch a stone pitcher of spring water for the use of the Hall tables.

The most impressive, but not reverential, service that came to my experience was that upon the visit of our beloved Queen Victoria and her … equally beloved husband, Albert the Good … in the October term, 1843. Oh! what inducements were held out to have King's boys transformed for a

short time. 'The Queen' would do this and that for them, 'The Queen' would speak to them, 'The Queen' would leave presents for them, what would 'The Queen' not do for them? We were drilled as follows:- Upon the first royal foot being raised to the steps leading from the ante-chapel to the organ screen a well twined in [tuned] chord was drawn from the organ above, and immediately every boy's head was bowed behind the desks, and a certain number of bars rest counted, when a second stronger chord was applied, and 'Up heads', or open cessame[sic]. They had passed, and were seated on the (throne) dais erected just at the back of the stalls ready for the service to begin.

52 A print representing the visit of Queen Victoria and Prince Albert to the Chapel in 1843. Photograph: The Cambridgeshire Collection.

53 The choristers dressed in their Eton suits, originating from the uniform still worn by pupils at Eton College. Photograph: © Hanya Chlala.

# In the 1920s

*Hilary Wayment, ch. 1922-5*

The chorister's life was tougher than it is now. There were no rest days, no services when only the men sang; and on Easter Day, for instance, there were three services instead of two. We had practices in the music room after breakfast, except on Sundays, when Dean Milner-White came for an hour's divinity, divinity full of warmth and humour. After lunch there was either a practice in the school, or a full practice with the men in the Chapel, about 4pm. I dreaded the school practices at first, for although I had a good ear I could often not sing the more difficult passages, and Dr. Mann would of course spot this, and make me try them alone. Once I dissolved in tears, but someone whispered to 'Daddy' Mann that I had had a letter that morning telling me of my grandmother's death (which was true, though as I scarcely knew her it had not made much impression). In a moment he was all sympathy and kindness, a side of his character unguessed at till then. I can see him still: a stocky man in a dark grey suit, arriving with a loose black cloak over his shoulders and a broad-brimmed black hat above his clipped, greying beard. He had made the Choir into what it was, and still is today. But in the early twenties there were no broadcasts, no recordings, no tours abroad, though already, immediately after the 1914-8 war, Milner-White had established the *Festival of Nine Lessons and Carols* at Christmas.

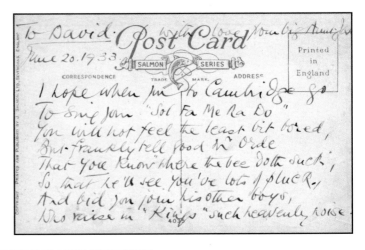

**54**  A good luck postcard sent to a chorister by his aunt.

**55**  Choristers' 'crocodile'. Photograph: Tim Rawle.

# In the 1950s

## *Rodney Williams, ch. 1952-5*

There were the Christmas parties and the staff 'panto' which the Headmaster, Donald Butters, wrote and acted in, always bringing in events and people known to the school and topical to the year ending. Boris Ord used to attend these and always entered into the fun with great relish. I remember him coming forward during the interval to play jazz with Hugh McLean [the then organ scholar] to our amazement and great delight—and he did it with great skill and vitality—fingers positively twinkling on the rather honky-tonk choir school piano!

I have treasured memories of Boris' Christmas Party with his sister Eve manning a huge blue enamelled teapot. Boris playing us Dr. Mann's '78' (Bach chorales) and allowing us to play with his famous collection of clockwork toys kept on the top of his two grand pianos (his and Dr. Mann's—back to back so he could play duets). The story goes that whenever Boris and John Dykes Bower (of St. Paul's) met they played the duet version of *The Arrival of the Queen of Sheba* and tried to break their own speed record without making a single mistake!!

**56** Choristers walking to Chapel. Photograph: Dona Haycraft.

**57** A letter sent to his parents by Clifford Mould, ch. 1954–8.

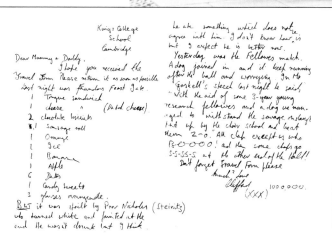

# In the 1990s

*Alastair Hussain, ch. 1991-6*

06:50   I am called to life by a matron and the member of staff on duty—the famous fanfare of 'Rise and shine, it's time to get up, time to get moving' trumpets aloud much to the boys' frustration!

(07:10-07:14)   Rise, get up and get moving.

07:15   Breakfast. By this time I should be washed, changed, and be ready for the day ahead of me. For breakfast we have a choice of three cereals and/or toast. On Sundays I also have a cooked breakfast: bacon & eggs etc.

07:30   Time for music practices. I play two instruments, the piano and double-bass. A student teacher comes round the practice rooms to check if we are practising and whether or not we need any help.

08:15   Chorister Practice. Every morning (except Sunday) I have a one hour long rehearsal taken by Mr. Cleobury and/or an organ scholar. This takes place in the 'Chorister room' and 'Probationer room', each with a grand piano. The chorister room also has stools and benches that we put our music on. All 16 choristers and six probationers take part. We practise all the music necessary for that week and coming concerts. We also learn about the composers and various aspects of the music that we are singing and involved with.

58   Choristers en route back to school from the Chapel. Photograph: *Times Newspapers.*

09:20   The start of the academic school day. At this point during the day I join forces with the rest of my form to start lessons. There are two forms in each year, and in the top year there is an added (academic) scholar-ship form. We study a range of subjects based on the national curriculum and each lesson (period) lasts 35 minutes.

(09:55) Start of second period.

10:30   Break. This is free time for the whole school in which I often have a 'break prac-tice' (sport) or musical commitments such as chamber music groups. At the start of every morning break we have a drink and biscuits: this is often when I meet other staff and pupils.

11:00-12:45  Lessons continue.

12:45   Lunch. Each year group goes to lunch at staggered intervals and has a choice of hot or cold meals and dessert. This is followed by a break in which I may have an orchestra rehearsal or chamber music. Most choristers play football or other sports such as tennis or basketball during these breaks.

13:40-15:00  Lessons resume.

15:10   Organised games start, taken by one of the sports teachers. I get an hour of games on Monday; twenty minutes on Tuesday;

a varied amount on Wednesday; an hour on Thursday and none on Friday.

15:30    Time to change. I change into Etons ready for the evening chapel routine. The more practice you get at changing into Etons, the faster you get. The older boys and matrons often have to lend a hand to the younger ones simply because these are so different from any other clothes you are ever likely to wear! An older boy may be able to change in two minutes whereas it may take a new boy ten. Etons consist of: pinstriped trousers; a pure white shirt with a separate collar which is held in place by a front and a back stud; a thick black tie; a black waistcoat; a short black jacket and a gown, similar to those worn in universities; and the famous Top Hat. The bottom button of the waistcoat is left undone by tradition: Edward VII once went to a public occasion but forgot to button his bottom button, and so people regarded this as fashion and did the same. This does sound bizarre but there seems little point in changing a tradition which we share with our sister school, Eton, where the waistcoats are made so that it is impossible to button-up the bottom button.

15:40    Little tea. This usually consists of a small cake and a drink. I often have my own 'tuck' (crisps, chocolate etc.) as well, so that I don't get hungry during the pre-evensong practice.

15:55    Croc out. The 'crocodile' of boys (eight pairs walking in a straight line) departs for Chapel. This is an almost ritual part of the day where I must respect 500-year-old rules and regulations during our procession-like walk to chapel: e.g. silence from the College gate. I must carry my own music in a black case. This is a famous spectacle for tourists to behold, not least for the sight of the 16 boys sporting the unique 'Top Hats'.

16:15    Evensong rehearsal begins. Before every service there is a rehearsal. This lasts for an hour and is similar to the morning practice except the choral scholars also take part.

17:15    Break. I have about twelve minutes to eat a cake, have a drink, change into cassock and surplice and line up to go through for the vestry prayer before we process into Chapel at 5.30pm, by which time we appear relaxed and calm.

18:15-18:30    Service ends. We hand in the completed music, change back into full Etons and 'croc' back to school where we have supper. After supper we have free time in which I generally play sport with the rest of the choristers and boarders.

20:00    Prep begins. This is the time in which we do homework set during the day. The older you are, the more homework you get.

20:30-20:45    Prep ends. Free time inside the boarding house begins, watching TV, playing pool etc.

21:00—21:35    Lights out. Having washed and changed, the older you are, the later you go to bed.

# A Lenten Prose

*Dominic Vlasto, ch. 1964-9*

For the visitor to Cambridge who happens to descend on King's College Chapel on Ash Wednesday or Good Friday, the singing of the *Miserere* by Allegri in such a setting must be a powerfully memorable event. In the vaulted candle-lit gloom of a February evening it seems as though such music and such a building become a single entity, indivisible in intent and effect, more than just 'made for each other', though indeed in a sense they were.

However, I suspect that even former choristers largely forget much of the routine of the daily round of practices and services which make up the largest and most important part of the Choir's life; and it is worth remembering that 'special' services like those on Ash Wednesday or Advent Sunday do not happen, and never did happen, without a good deal of meticulous preparation that is woven into the structure of the normal term-time day.

The day's rehearsals begin at 8.15am in the chorister block at the School, a functional, rather bare room whose focus is the piano, round which are ranged three long choir desks at which the boys perch on high stools. The routine business of daily practice starts with opening the lungs and stretching the vocal chords. All throats now cleared and minds focused, the work begins. Not Allegri yet, because much of the rest of the day's very full programme must also be attended to.

About half of the sixty-minute practice passes before the Allegri is even opened, and then the proceedings start with a relaxing joke about another choir Stephen knows which 'always cheats, and does it down a semitone'. The choice of the *favoriti*—the four boys who will take the two treble lines in the semi-chorus—is delayed until Stephen has had more chances to listen carefully to who may be in particularly good (or bad) voice that day, and for some time various combinations are tried. (It is in truth as much a Latin lesson as a music practice, as the meaning and emphasis of the words is always examined before singing them with the music.) Finally the moment comes when serious decisions have to be taken. 'Who feels up to those top Cs?' Almost every hand shoots up. Typically, the one senior boy whose hand didn't shoot up (one of the cold-nursers) was chosen to try out first, then one by one six or seven others, including several relatively young ones, one of whom is dismissed encouragingly with the thought that 'that'll be alright in a year's time'. A pause. There is almost a holding breath, and then Stephen quietly but decisively announces the selection: the senior and second-senior chorister to take the top and second line respectively, and each of them supported by another younger boy. For an instant there is the merest suggestion of a Macaulay Culkin-style 'Yesss!' from those chosen …

The start of the afternoon practice in the Chapel is a model of efficiency, with every single member of the choir sorting themselves out without fuss and the music all laid out in the choir stalls by the boys whose job it is. At four o'clock precisely Stephen is just there, steps up to the conductor's desk, says 'Thank you very much', and at once all is attention and the practice has started dead on time.

The service music is worked through in order, though the Allegri, despite filling the role of Introit, is again left until last. When the moment comes for them all to tumble from the choir stalls to practise and choreograph the Allegri, they make their way to the west end, the *favoriti* to a side-chapel and the cantor to the organ-loft.

The habit nowadays is for the *favoriti* to sing from behind almost completely closed doors. It certainly makes for a very distant and ethereal effect from wherever you hear it, even from near the choir stalls. It also means, I suppose, that those on the spot don't have to be quite so subtle or nurse their high Cs with great tenderness, and from very close range it is apparent that they are actually singing it quite

**59** The boys have their early morning practice in the chorister block at school. Photograph: Penny Cleobury.

loudly. They are so distant from the main body of the Choir that it is impossible for their conductor to know exactly what is going on at this point of the practice without an extra helper, which is why both organ scholars are in attendance.

A moment later, the side-chapel is once again cool, clean and intimate as the *favoriti* vanish to re-join the main body of the Choir, by now just on the ante-chapel side of the screen, and the final chorus is run through twice, the first time being 'pretty appalling', with all exhorted to 'listen to the others: listen, tune and blend'. At 5.13pm, after a final reminder from Stephen about the order of the music, they are dismissed, and come trotting back into the stalls to do the final bits of organisation before the hordes are let in.

For those coming to King's for the first time, or seldom, listening to the actual performance in the service must be an almost shattering experience which lingers in the memory. For the boys, however, there is not much thought beyond the immediate concern of turning in a decent performance. Theirs is a busy and organised life which is lived very much with the moment, and there's little room for looking backwards, whether from regret or pride. There's a chance to unwind with one's parents, if they've been able to come, on the walk back down the avenue and up West Road back to the School, and then it's straight back into the next school thing, which is probably Prep.

And the next day begins, as normal, with scales at 8.15am and another batch of psalms, anthems and introits to be polished and refined before school starts. It's simply another routine day of efficient musical accomplishment, and they know that they will be expected to be businesslike and professional about it, whatever is on the service-sheet.

© Dominic Vlasto, 1997

**60** During the past four years the Choir has recorded some of the great choral works on video with Columns Classics. Clockwise from top left, the pictures are from recordings of: *Messiah, St Matthew Passion, Israel in Egypt* (in costume as Hebrew slaves) and *St John Passion*. Photographs: Columns Classics.

## Holy Week Impressions

*Christopher Chivers, c.t. 1989-94*

If the Rubens adds poignancy to the Christmas celebrations at King's, in Holy Week it is the stained glass which provides a matchless window onto the mystery of salvation. Indeed, as the altar is stripped at the end of the Eucharist on Maundy Thursday, and the Rubens is closed-off from view, what is left is the stark reality of the Passion story which the windows narrate. The re-strained exuberance of Josquin's *Missa Pange Lingua*, sung to celebrate the institution of the Communion at the Last Supper, gives way to the meditative simplicity of Victoria's Passion, sung the following morning when the Cross is venerated. Even the haunting beauty of the treble soloist in Allegri's *Miserere* cannot transcend the despair and forsakenness which pervades the Chapel.

At the School, a Passover Supper, which the choristers delight in cooking themselves—a solemn yet colourful occasion—similarly contrasts with their dramatic re-enactment of soldiers nailing the Nazarene to the Cross—at which many young eyes fill with tears. Palm-cross making and the baking of hot-cross buns are engaging, even enjoyable activities, but they are always hedged about with questions. 'Do you think that anyone should be enjoying themselves on Good Friday?', one concerned 11-year-old asks. 'Why is it a *Good* Friday?', enquires another. As evening draws in, we walk the Stations of the Cross in a dormitory, and close with candlelit Compline. A profound sense of awe has an almost tangible quality to it, as choristers settle to sleep.

If Good Friday had been a day of prolonged emotional intensity, Holy Saturday brings with it intensity of a different kind, through the concentration required to sing the exacting vocal lines of a Bach *Passion*. But there is also a sense of anticipation of what will follow, as the nuanced grace of a Mozart Mass receives final rehearsal for Easter morning.

**61** During Lent the cross is shrouded. Photograph: Penny Cleobury.

**62** In the Good Friday morning service the Dean proclaims 'Behold the Cross' and the shroud is removed. Photograph: Penny Cleobury.

**63** On Easter morning the Paschal candle is lit. Photograph: Penny Cleobury.

Sublime though the Bach *Passions* are, they are also very lengthy: an exhausting sing for all concerned. 'But Jesus was on the Cross for nine hours, sir. We're exhausted after three', one chorister observes. His remark seems to put everything into perspective.

Easter Sunday dawns, as spring-flowers line the crocodile's route to the Chapel, and choristers cheerfully contemplate the eating of all the eggs which they have collected in an early-morning hunt around the School! Charles Wood's *This joyful Eastertide* signals the start of the liturgical celebrations, which continue unabated, as a packed Chapel greets the Risen Lord. Shafts of bright sunlight pierce through the glass, transcending the sufferings of crucifixion. The angels on the organ screen trumpet the empty tomb. He is risen indeed. Alleluia!

## Directing Collegium Regale

*Thomas Elias, ch. 1983-6, c.s. 1992-5*

Directing Collegium Regale, you might think, should be a trivial matter of waving your hands around in the air a bit during concerts, and receiving an extra credit in the programme. This is, of course, true. Unfortunately, in the small print are sundry other titles which are acquired by default: Librarian, Secretary, Nanny, Amateur Photocopier Repairman, and the prestigious position of Keeper of the Pencils. Before the beginning of the year, in order to find new music which will keep audiences amused and the group fresh, you encourage, beg, cajole, bribe and generally pledge everlasting gratitude to anyone who is prepared to write new close-harmony arrangements. Desiring only a quiet life, such friends as you can find promise to write arrangements—and then proceed to vanish. A fortnight or so later, and they begin to skulk in corners and hurry past you with hunched shoulders. If approached in conciliatory mood, excuses pour guiltily forth: 'I've actually finished it, it's all in my head. I just haven't got round to writing it out yet', or more realistically, 'I know. I know. Sorry. Sorry. Next Tuesday. Definitely.' It is clear at this point that they have yet to make a start on the promised music.

During this period—since all your friends are avoiding you—time should be profitably spent in finding music for other parts of the programme. This is the moment to investigate the Collegium Regale Library. This sounds very elegant, and conjures up images of oak bookstacks, Afghan rugs, and deferential lighting caressing dusky tomes of leather-bound vellum. Reality, however, has different ideas. The 'Library' consists of five large cardboard boxes, in which sacred songs and profane madrigals jostle for stave room, before spreading out to cover every available surface in your room, blatantly contravening half-a-dozen arcane fire regulations. Leafing half-heartedly through this forest of missing pages, the conclusion is rapidly reached that this music's unsuitability is matched only by its illegibility. The Library, in fact, seems to have no useful function, apart from making otherwise empty cupboards feel wanted. Some hardy souls respond to the challenge enthusiastically, delving into obscure volumes to rescue forgotten masterpieces by Hassler, Gombert, or Osbert Parsley. Many such masterpieces were, however, forgotten for good reason. Others find genuinely interesting additions to the repertoire—Finnish part songs by Toivo Kuula were well received by audiences, while providing something distinctly different (read 'unpronounceable') for the performers.

When not finding music for such diverse occasions as concerts in churches, entertainment after dinner, and carols in the pub, the first couple of weeks of the year are filled with fairly intensive rehearsals, as the group learns four or five numbers off by heart. This is not as bad as it sounds, as few members of the group seem to pay too much attention to the notes in the first place. The director of

'Coll Reg' however becomes the universal conscience of the group: in a masterly display of double-think, he has to encourage and threaten the others to learn the music properly, even while he is vainly grasping for the notes himself. Removing the copies, however, dramatically improves the performance of the group, as they have to communicate directly with the audience—there is nowhere to hide. While this improves standards in concert, off-stage it becomes almost as important. On tour, we usually get mistaken for a football team, an illusion quickly dispelled when we get anywhere near a ball. Once it turns out that we are a choir, however, everyone wants a song at short notice. 'Coll Reg' frequently sings as a 'thank-you' at parties, or provides encores after full choir concerts. 'Happy Birthday' was once sung to a very embarrassed girl in-flight to Australia, and the group often sings simply for its own amusement, despite peculiar glances from confused onlookers.

　　With the programme decided and the music arranged, the actual conducting of the group seems comparatively simple. With the group consisting of 14 singers, however, every musical question provokes 15 opinions. Sorry, that should

**64**　Montage: During the spring holiday, Collegium Regale splits into two groups of seven men and tours the North and South of Britain.
Photographs:
1-5 Jonathan Rippon;
6,7 Richard Eteson.

be 14 opinions and one valid musical interpretation, which is, of course yours. Somehow, not everyone sees it that way, and bargaining becomes the indispensable tool. The baritones may compromise on the phrasing of one line, the first altos may be persuaded to abandon their firmly held belief that 'it is better to be sharp than out of tune', but mere words cannot persuade second tenors to sing top As quietly. Especially in close-harmony numbers, the style and mood of individual pieces is largely determined by the soloist. The conductor's role is frequently reduced to that of spoilsport: just as people are beginning to enjoy themselves, he has to persuade them to listen to niggling little details about it being out of time, out of tune, or just out of control. Frank Sinatra may have done it His Way; the director of 'Coll Reg' has to be more diplomatic.

## Hosting a Visit from Collegium Regale
### *Patricia Roberts*

What goes through the mind when, for the first time, Collegium Regale arrives to give a concert in the local church? I know that they will arrive in time for a light tea, after which I shall show them to their accommodation for the night, and that they will have supper with me after the concert and retire to bed after a suitable interval. Beyond that I have just my imagination to support me. I have prepared the supper and made sandwiches for tea together with fruit cakes. I know that King's College, Cambridge is a prestigious foundation, so I assume the Scholars will be equally superior. Is the cottage tidy and clean? I ask my husband to ensure that newspapers, books, unanswered letters and advertising leaflets are all put away out of sight and say to him 'please will you just Hoover through before they are due to arrive from their previous venue at about 3.30pm?'. I am surprised when a rather battered old minibus pulls into my yard and seven young men tumble out with nondescript luggage. Not a necktie in sight. Can this really be Collegium Regale? It is! They demolish all the sandwiches and cake and proceed to lie all over my floor to watch England play some foreigners (the home team win and I am fearful that my neighbours will complain at the whoops of joy from my cottage). Then *Home and Away* and *Neighbours*. Do undergraduates really watch such rubbish? I rush down to the Church to make sure that all is in order and leave my husband to clear up. What a gem, he does not complain. I can hardly believe my eyes when I next see the choir. They are beautifully dressed for the performance. Are they the same young men that I saw an hour ago? After the concert I rush off to lay up the hot buffet supper, and make sure that the white wine is properly chilled and the red wine is at room temperature. My husband checks the stock of canned beer. 'No problem darling, there is enough for me and they will drink wine I am sure.' I have invited a few friends of my generation to leaven the bread and they drift in after the concert. The choir also drift in after having visited the pub, and invite all and sundry to help themselves from the dining-room table. My friends get stuck into the wine and my husband is dismayed that the choir mainly elect to drink beer. Adequate stock of beer? You must be joking! Everyone is happy and talking madly. My gem of a husband rushes round making sure that all our guests are replete with alcohol before he eats. Eat? It has all been eaten. No beer left and no food left except a lump of cheese in the fridge. And so to bed. In the morning (or rather very late morning) a group of bleary eyed choral scholars assembles to load the minibus and we wave goodbye. The superior scholars have become normal but delightful young men and I think how nice it would be if my daughter would take up with one of them.

**65** (overleaf)  The Choir in the Chapel. Photograph: Eaden Lilley (Photography)

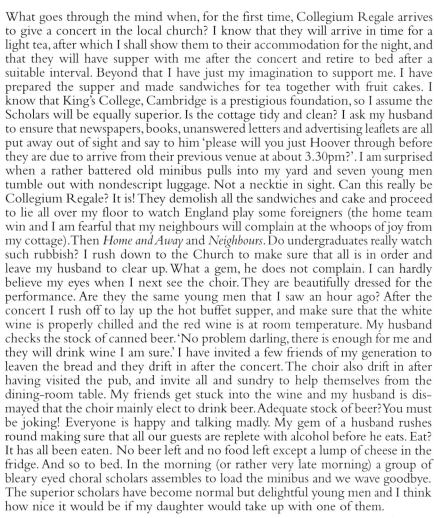

*Chapter Five*

# EASTER TERM

67

## Easter
*George Pattison*

A garden, in springtime: any garden, any springtime, and a score of images that speak to us of renewal and rebirth. Cambridge is a city of gardens and a city that is at its most beautiful in the early weeks of spring. The avenue leading from the Backs into King's is a sea of wild flowers, and across the meadow, cherry and almond trees are heavy with blossom. How apt that the most evocative of all the gospel stories about Easter is set in a garden, when Mary Magdalene (known in legend as the woman who was the sinner, to whom much had been forgiven because she loved much) meets the Risen Lord, at first failing to recognise Him and knowing Him only when He speaks to her by name. This is also the subject of one of the most dramatic of all the images in the Chapel windows, one that shows Mary in that moment of recognition. She is portrayed with a fluidity and a passion that belongs to the Baroque more than to the Middle Ages: here is a living, feeling human being in the rapture of a moment in which fear and longing, love and awe are altogether fused. She is totally transfixed, totally given over to all that is happening in this earth-shaking, history-changing encounter. The beauty of the garden fades into the background and we are faced with the realisation that if we are to know the meaning of the Easter gospel then we too must be transformed as profoundly as she.

**66** A section of Chapel window no.17, showing Mary Magdalene meeting the Risen Christ on Easter morning. Photograph: College Library.

**68** Montage: The Choral Scholars are undergraduates at King's College, reading for degrees in various subjects. Photographs: 1,5 Jonathan Rippon; 3, Richard Eteson; 2,4,6,7,8, Penny Cleobury.

# A Matron's View
## *Dorothy Roberts, former matron, 1980-93*

Being a Matron for the choristers has lots of responsibilities, and being there when a chorister sings his first service or solo is one of the highlights after the mundane jobs.

### Sick Bay and Surgery

One of matron's main responsibilities is keeping the choristers healthy as well as happy. Surgery for day to day medications and accidents. Sick Bay when a few days in bed are needed. There, some tender loving care from matron, also some extra company and sympathy from Henri, matron's cat, soon do the trick!

**69**   A chorister in 'Sick Bay' has a visit from Matron's cat. Photograph: Dorothy Roberts.

### Michaelmas Term

Probationers becoming choristers; choristers who have grown upwards and, in some cases, outwards need new Eton suits. Older choristers thinking it is a bit of a bore yet again having to be refitted into Etons. Laughter when the youngest chorister needs one of the larger top hats. Thank goodness services don't start until the University term begins. Plenty of time to fit cassocks and surplices as well.

Christmas is coming—lovely music and carols. Wonderful 'hums' from the bathrooms. Christmas also means stockings and presents from the College. Lists to Matron by Half Term. This gives Matron time to have the fun of buying all the odds and ends. The boys get some things that they have asked for without knowing exactly which presents from their original list are in the stocking.

### Lent Term

Music scholarships for choristers in their last year. Top probationers having a chance to sing in a service. Youngest choristers having a chance to sing a solo! 'Will you ring and let my mother know, Matron? I know she won't be able to come, but I just want her to know, even if it is only three notes!'

The ethereal notes of Allegri's *Miserere* or the *Pie Jesu* coming out of the bathroom.

What, no cake? I have given it up for Lent, but not down in the vestry.

Easter eggs—a hunt on Grantchester meadows; let's hope it doesn't rain.

Easter morning—wonderful service and music, followed by chocolate down Eton suits!

### Summer Term

Common Entrance exams for all leavers. Choristers hoping to back up their music scholarships. [Many choristers gain music awards to their next school but still have to pass the required entrance exam.]

Cricket matches, followed by a race to change into Etons. 'Do we have to wear jackets? It is so hot!'

The tour in the summer holidays—'Will my voice last? Matron, I have started to croak!'

# May Week

May week (usually the second week in June!) celebrates the end of exams and the Easter Term, with concerts, plays, garden parties and balls. Collegium Regale often sing at several May Balls which means that little sleep is had during the week!

**70**   The Choir takes part in the College May Week concert which is followed by wine with strawberries and cream on the Back Lawn. This is much enjoyed by everyone, but especially the choristers. Photograph: Peter Tregear.

**71** (left)   This photograph was taken at the King's May Ball of 1939. Boris Ord can be seen in the first seated row towards the right. Photograph: The Cambridgeshire Collection.

**72** (above)   Jonathan Rippon (centre) and friends at a May Ball in 1993. Photograph: Jonathan Rippon.

# A Piece of Cake

*John Boulter, Chapel Administrator, 1990-*

'What is it today, Mr. B.?'

'J.Ds.'

'Yessss!'

Many people are overawed when they learn that I work in King's College Chapel, and have some involvement with the Choir. The reality is not so impressive. I provide the vestments, fitting and repairing cassocks or hurriedly replacing surplices stained by such things as a nose-bleed; pencils for marking music copies. I attempt to keep the vestries tidy: not easy as they are used by over thirty people. I attempt to keep choristers and candles apart—are all boys aged nine to 13 pyromaniacs? I even occasionally become Mr. Mop, clearing up the results of the latest tummy bug.

However, I am left in little doubt as to my most important task as Chapel Administrator. Nothing to do with preparing for the services or concerts, the maintenance of the building or accommodating the thousands of visitors. No. It is the selection of cakes for the Choir's tea-break between practice and service.

After the failure of several bakeries to guarantee satisfaction, this onerous responsibility has fallen to me. And onerous responsibility it is. Choose the right varieties and all is harmony (sorry!), but get it wrong and complaints pour in from several directions: 'flapjacks are boring'; 'coconut tarts are disgusting'; 'the jam went over their surplices'; 'the chocolate melted on to their Eton jackets'. Will an unfed Choir survive hunger and last through the service?

Thus I have to take the choice seriously. The sight of this sober suited man carefully selecting up to seventy five cakes does not pass without comment in Marks and Spencer's food hall or Nadia's patisserie. Many fellow shoppers have invited themselves to tea with me or wondered how I stay so slim.

So back to the 'J.Ds' in the conversation at the beginning. They are, of course, the ever popular jam doughnuts. Thank goodness there's no reproof today and evensong can go ahead with a suitably nourished choir. I don't know about an army marching but I like to think that, to some extent at least, a choir sings on its stomach.

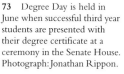

**73** Degree Day is held in June when successful third year students are presented with their degree certificate at a ceremony in the Senate House. Photograph: Jonathan Rippon.

*Chapter Six*

# LONG VACATION TERM

75

## The West Window
*George Pattison*

The West Window is the poor relation of the Chapel windows, being a 19th-century addition from which purists turn aside. Yet it is splendid in its own right and was the occasion of one of my most memorable moments in King's. Many years ago, before the advent of the Chapel Shop, concert orchestras and choirs were seated below the window, with the audience facing them, that is, facing the west end of the Chapel. On this occasion we had gone to attend a performance of Beethoven's *Missa Solemnis* which took place on a summer's evening. As the sun went down the angle of the light was continually changing and each change seemed to illuminate a different range of colours: now reds, then greens, next mauve and culminating in a blaze of gold before finally fading into dusk. The dramatic play of colour seemed to interpret the drama of music and word in a new and surprising way. If such is the aesthetic foretaste, what will the reality be?

74 The West window of King's College Chapel dates from 1879. Photograph: James Austin by kind permission of Douglas Morgan

76 Montage: Choir recording. King's College Choir has become known throughout the world through its recordings with HMV, Decca and EMI. The first record was issued in 1930 (from a session in 1927). Through records we are able to hear the different qualities brought to the choir by successive Directors of Music. Photographs: 1, 4, 8, © Hanya Chlala; 2, in which Peter Maxwell Davies is on the left, Judy Arnold; 6, Simon Eadon; 3, 5, 7, © EMI Records Ltd.

## The Long Vacation Term

✧

During July and August some students are in Cambridge for special courses of study and research. The Choir sings for a three-week period during this time.

## Diary of a Chorister Mother

*Sue Eadon, chorister parent*

✧

### The Voice Trial

Our son has been elected to a choristership—GREAT, WONDERFUL, PANIC!—is it what he wants? Is it what we want? With other children is it a commitment we can all make? Son so determined this is right for him that we accept. Everyone at the school was incredibly helpful and forthcoming and this mother was able to start her first-born off feeling as much preparation had been done as possible.

## The First Year

Leaving son at school much easier than expected—certainly for him! First couple of days he found very strange, but then that would happen at any new school. The staff are obviously aware of this and do keep a special eye on new boarders. We were only a phone call away (the boys have their own call box) and furnished with a phonecard from us he was able to ring whenever he wanted to. Also in his first year he was able to come home most week-ends. House staff most approachable if one still had any worries or questions.

The rest of the year continued happily with him amazingly (to us!) managing to cope with practice and prep without parental supervision, and usually remembering to be in the right place at the right time. My one moment of major angst was when my eight-year-old first went into sick bay—I felt it was too young not to be looked after by me; he thought it was great: 'It's alright Mummy, there's *lots* of Lego, a video recorder, and Matron brings us meals in bed!'

## The Second Year

Two weeks of term pass and eventually the first service arrives, fortunately on a Saturday. I go to see the 'croc' [choristers walk from school to Chapel in pairs like a crocodile] out. My son, usually to be found in a rugger shirt and grubby, patched jeans when out of school uniform, emerges transformed into a King's chorister dressed in Eton suit.

At last his first service. I find the seats reserved for chorister parents. I watch the smallest chorister in the Cantoris choir stalls and burst with pride. To be honest he looked petrified throughout the service!

Christmas approaches—two concerts in London, TV recording, recording sessions and home for a short week-end. We talk about whether he is looking forward to Christmas—he isn't, mainly because he doesn't really know what to expect—I admit to similar feeling.

I really shouldn't have worried. He had the most wonderful Choir Time: skating, cooking, drama sessions, going to the pantomime, and many other activities in between Choir practices. Christmas Eve came and parents started arriving around late morning to take turns queueing outside Chapel and in a College room get-

77   During the Long Vacation the gentlemen from St John's Choir play the gentlemen of King's Choir at cricket. This light-hearted game can sport some creative scoring! Photograph: Penny Cleobury.

ting into the swing of Christmas. Eventually we were allowed in to Chapel for the live broadcast. After years of listening to it on the radio while peeling potatoes, it was like a dream come true. I really couldn't believe my son was part of those soaring descants (I still can't). After the service the Choir and their families repaired to College for an excellent tea. Later the Choristers and their families returned to school for family entertainment and supper. By now I really was beginning to feel part of a much larger family beyond the one I was born into or married to. Eventually it was time for the boys to go to bed and the rest of us to leave. Next morning we all reconvened in Chapel for the morning service—parents and boys looking bright-eyed and bushy-tailed, staff looking distinctly jaded—what had the little rascals been up to?! Christmas lunch at School—if anyone had ever told me I'd have school lunch on Christmas Day I'd have laughed, but it seemed such a natural thing to do, and for the choristers there was the added excitement of this also being the start of the holidays.

The Easter term started with son being much more relaxed about everything. School Easter holidays start but Choir stays back for recording sessions, then home for a few days and back again to Cambridge for Easter Choir Time. There are more services than at Christmas, but no television or radio broadcasts. We are now beginning to take this slightly strange way of life in our stride.

The Summer Term starts with more thought about the cricket season than singing! School Summer holidays start and the Choir stay back to finish the term's services. Home for a few days then off on Tour to … Australia! Son was by now just ten and away on the other side of the world for two and a half weeks. It seemed longer to me and he might have been on another planet for all I knew, but we did have a few phone calls from him and he was obviously having a wonderful time with all the families he was billeted with, some of whom clearly took great trouble to make it a memorable experience.

Their return plane landed at Heathrow at 6.30am and most of the parents were there to meet it—I've no idea what the rest of the terminal made of this large group of excited middle-aged people swapping news of various phone calls with their sons. Finally the boys arrived through customs clearly having slept in their school uniform. Son was tired but on a high from the entire experience—for once he appreciated coming home, boomerangs and all!

78   King's Choir joins with the St John's College Choir to sing an Evensong each July. The venue alternates between the two college chapels. Photograph: Penny Cleobury.

**79** Collegium Regale provides the entertainment at a huge charity event held each summer just outside Cambridge at Childerley Hall. Each year around six hundred people listen to the group sing in a huge barn and then picnic in the beautiful grounds. Photograph: Penny Cleobury.

## The Third Year

Son is now starting to look as if he was born into choristership. I really can't believe how happy, settled and on top of everything he is now. A recent conversation with him went something like this:

Mother:              'Do you want to come round to the Smiths with us for tea?'
Son:                    'No thanks. I'd rather muck about at home on my bicycle.'
Mother (wailing):  'Home?'
Son:                    'Oh sorry! School.'

I reflect that since becoming a chorister nearly two years ago he has spent only 13 complete weeks and seven half weeks at home. I sadly accept his slip of the tongue, and realise why I feel every moment spent with him is so precious. He has loosened the apron strings rather earlier than I was ready for, but it's my problem, not his—he is clearly doing something he feels passionate about: singing in King's College Chapel.

**80** Prince Philip leading the procession from the Senate House following the Honorary Degree ceremony. Photograph: *Cambridge Evening News.*

## Honorary Degrees

✧

Each summer Cambridge University honours eight people, distinguished in many different walks of life, with an Honorary Degree. The ceremony, performed by Prince Philip as Chancellor of the University, takes place in the Senate House. The two choirs of King's and St John's provide the music on this special occasion.

# Leaving the Choir

*Anon.*

Anyone who has had the privilege of singing in the Choir of King's College at Cambridge as a choral scholar or a chorister, or who has been one of its organ scholars, will have poignant memories of his last Service in the Chapel. He cannot have spent at such an impressionable age three years, sometimes four, whether in the College or its School, bonded in pursuit of the highest standards in performance, working with the utmost dedication, often for as many as three or four hours a day, on our extraordinary repertoire in one of the world's most beautiful buildings, without being most profoundly affected by the experience. Not surprisingly many are visibly moved, when it all comes to an end, by the finality of the occasion, reflecting that they may never again in their lives, unless they are one of a very small number of choristers destined to return to the Choir as choral scholars five or six years later, take part in an endeavour that requires such commitment, demonstrates such collegiality and achieves such remarkable results. All are deeply grateful for the opportunities they have had of singing the daily services in the Chapel, of performing in concerts, of broadcasting, of making recordings and of taking part in overseas tours.

Many will seek to keep in touch with each other and will return from time to time to hear the Choir, which they will point out was always at its best in their day!

Some will take up careers as professional musicians, whether as singers, instrumentalists, conductors and choirmasters, and just as their lives have been touched by the tradition of 500 years, so they will in their music-making touch the lives of others. But wherever former members of the Choir find themselves and in whatever profession, surely their overwhelming sentiment will be a sense of pride in having been part of all this.

**81** The Director of Music asks the leaving choristers what music they would like to sing at Evensong on the last Saturday of Long Vac. Term; likewise he asks the leaving choral scholars to select the music for the final Evensong on Sunday afternoon. At the end of that Evensong, the West door of the Chapel is open and for several members of the Choir each year it signifies their going out into the wider world, after their time in King's Choir. Photograph: Penny Cleobury.

*Chapter Seven*

# TOURS

## Choir tours abroad

✧

King's College Choir went on its first foreign tour as far back as 1936. Sixty years on, we are used to college, and indeed school, groups travelling the world. Unlike other choirs, King's only has the opportunity to undertake one major tour every year, due to daily services, Christmas and Easter commitments, and the educational needs of its schoolboys and undergraduate students.

In 1936 one of the choristers, now 'Captain' Maurice Willey, kept a diary of his first trip and the following extract gives an insight into early expeditions abroad.

**82** The choristers on the deck of the SS *Vienna* sailing to Holland. Photograph: Maurice Willey.

## The first foreign tour 1936
*Maurice Willey, ch. 1932-8*

On 9 December 1935, the Dean, Eric Milner-White, wrote to parents of the choristers to announce that the College had been approached by the Foreign Office on behalf of the British Council to discover if it would be willing 'in the national interest' to allow the Choir to sing in Amsterdam, Copenhagen, Stockholm and 'not more than one or two other places'. He explained that no promise of acceptance had been given at that stage, pending parents' indication of willingness to permit their sons to participate in the tour, adding the observation that the College was anxious to make the project a 'holiday with a little singing' and hoped that the boys, young as they were, would gain both 'instruction and amusement …'

## Itinerary (outward)

Cambridge—Harwich—Hook of Holland—The Hague—Amsterdam—Hamburg—Copenhagen—Malmo—Lund—Stockholm—Uppsala.

The Choir, and other senior members of the College left Cambridge station on their first and arguably momentous visit abroad on 19 March 1936, with 15 boys, choral scholars, Boris Ord, Dean Milner-White, and C. M. Fiddian, Headmaster of the School.

The only nervous member of the party appeared, in fact, to be the Headmaster who was observed pacing the deck of SS *Vienna* in search of a suitable niche near a ventilator! After settling in at The Hague, the first practice of the tour took place in the Dutch Reformed Church.

When the Choir gave its first performance, the Dutch showed considerable appreciation. So much so, in fact, that some were observed pipe-smoking during the service! A recording was made which was to be broadcast later. A relatively short journey saw the Choir at Amsterdam where it sang again in the evening.

While in Copenhagen the Choir carried out two engagements; the first at a church where an evening service was given before an appreciative congregation. The following day (25 March) a well-received concert was given at a museum.

Leaving Copenhagen on 26 March en-route to Malmo involved a short sea route and then on to Lund. The Swedish Press appeared bemused, apparently

**83** The Choir at Copenhagen station. Photograph: Dansk Presse Foto.

**84**   The Choir at an evening concert in Copenhagen in March 1936. Photograph: Unknown.

anticipating a royal arrival in the shape of the King's Choir; some enquired whether the King had arrived with his choir, and if so, where was he? It was explained that the Dean was leading the party and he was thus tentatively asked: 'We gather you are a King ...?' The Dean's reply was ... 'er–er–er– of King's!'

Lund Cathedral was the setting for further choral singing in the evening. On Saturday 28 March the Choir gave a recital in the Engelbretskyrkan. While based in Stockholm, the Choir paid a visit to Uppsala, where it was to perform in the Cathedral, and indeed be heard over the air in the UK. Its final engagement on Tuesday 31 March took place at St Jakobikirche, where the atmosphere was enhanced by the reminder that J. S. Bach himself once played on the organ there. And so ended the Choir's first foreign tour as it left Hamburg Central Station for the Hook of Holland on Wednesday 1 April 1936.

A suitable epilogue can be found in a letter to *The Times* by Dean Milner-White which appeared on 21 April 1936:

'... On its own small scale, the Choir's tour was unique in the story of five nations ... at the separate request of each city, the Recital of Motets was prefaced by Evensong, given in no wise as a Concert but as a service, exactly as in Chapel in Cambridge ...'

**85**   The choristers in Copenhagen in March 1996. Photograph: Penny Cleobury.

**86** Choir Tour photographs from Africa. 1. The choristers at Cape of Good Hope; 2. The Choir perform in Durban Town Hall; 3. The Choir in Lagos, Nigeria; 4. Choristers with a Zulu warrior; 5. The Choir sang in Soweto with a local choir; 6. The present headmaster at a safari park near Johannesburg. Photographs: 1, Andrew Corbett; 2,4,5, 6, Penny Cleobury; 3, Nigerian Ministry of Information.

**87** Choir Tour photographs from Australia. (Spot the author on the set of 'Neighbours'.) Photographs: 2,6, Jonathan Rippon; 1,3,5, Penny Cleobury; 4, Unknown.

**88** Choir Tour photographs from Europe. No. 3 shows the view from the Berlin Wall; no. 5 is a group shot taken before boarding Eurostar. Photographs: 1,6, Christopher Zealley; 2,5, Jonathan Rippon; 3,4,7,8, Penny Cleobury.

**89** Choir Tour photographs from Japan. Photographs: 2,5,6, Gerald Peacocke; 1,3,4,7, Penny Cleobury.

**90** Choir Tour photographs from the USA. Photographs: 2,4,5,8, Gerald Peacocke; 6, Elke Pollard; 7, Jonathan Rippon; 1,3, Penny Cleobury.

*Chapter Eight*

# REMINISCENCES

*David Willcocks, o.s. 1939-40 & 1945-7; O. & D. of M. 1957-73*

✧

1938   My first experience of the King's College Choir was when I was auditioned and interviewed for the Mann Organ Scholarship which was due to become vacant in September 1939. I felt reasonably confident over the tests at the organ, as I had had the chance to practise in the Chapel on the previous evening. It was the final test that remains in my memory... for it was taking a short rehearsal of the full Choir. I cannot remember what the anthem was, but the Choir seemed to sing it absolutely perfectly; the tone was beautiful, the intonation was secure, the parts well balanced, the phrasing sensitive. I had never experienced such beautiful singing before. As we approached the end of the anthem I suddenly felt terrified, because I knew that I was going to have to say something in a few seconds time... not only to the Choir, but to the shadowy gowned figures peering at me from the candlelit Fellows' stalls. Speaking in as bold a manner as I could under the circumstances, I told the Choir that the performance was quite creditable and had some good features, but that we would all work during the next ten to fifteen minutes to eliminate some of the weaknesses. I then asked if any boy could guess what were the weaknesses to which I was referring. To my great relief some hands shot up and various suggestions were put forward ... 'the performance could have had more variety, sir' ... 'weren't the tenors too loud on page two, sir?' ... 'the final 't' was not *quite* together, sir'. I deemed it unwise to open up the discussion to the choral scholars but told them that I presumed that they would not be uncomfortable if we sang the anthem a semi-tone higher in order to achieve a different 'colour'. We then sang through the anthem again, and apart from the change in pitch it was neither better nor worse, but I was congratulated by the Provost on a very imaginative rehearsal and the Dean thought that the anthem sounded quite different the second time. That evening I was informed that I had been elected to the organ scholarship, and so my long and happy association with King's began.

1939-40   I suppose that the most vivid memories of my first year at King's focus on the personality of Boris Ord who had been Fellow and Organist of the College since 1929. He was one of the finest musicians that I have ever encountered, setting for himself, and for those with whom he worked, the highest standards.

One particular memory I have is of playing for the Christmas Eve Carol Service in 1939. It was customary in those days for there to be one, two, or three minutes of complete silence preceding the opening of *Once in Royal David's City*, rather than 'doodling' on the organ in G major or a related key until the BBC red light began to flash. As soon as the red light became steady, Boris Ord would pluck a tuning fork and hold it to his ear, following which he would hum a note of indeterminate pitch, but vaguely centred on the D below middle C. It demanded nerves of steel on the part of the solo boy to embark with confidence on the first verse of the hymn, and the organ scholar always hoped to be spared the agonising decision whether to 'creep in' during verse three or four, or plunge in boldly with a gathering note before either of those verses.

1940-5   In June 1940 both Boris Ord and I left King's for war service. During his absence Boris Ord's place was taken by Dr. Harold Darke. Despite the difficulties of dealing with a choir of which the personnel was changing rapidly, Harold Darke maintained a very good standard and both Boris Ord and I found little difficulty in identifying the choir which at 3pm every Christmas Eve during the years of World War II broadcast *A Festival of Nine Lessons and Carols* from a 'college chapel'. For security reasons the precise location of broadcast events was never revealed on the air!

1945-7   Harold Darke remained in charge of the Choir until Christmas 1945, and he invited Boris Ord to play for the Christmas Eve Service, and he asked me to play for the Advent Carol Service, which was attended by Herbert Howells, who had been in charge of the St John's College Choir during the absence on war service of Dr. (later Professor) Robin Orr. I shall never forget the performance of *A Spotless Rose* at that Advent Carol Service.

1957-73   In 1957 it became evident to the Provost and the College Council that Boris Ord would not be able to carry on much longer, owing to a progressive illness from which there was then no proven cure. I was accordingly appointed to succeed him as Organist from September 1957, it being understood that he should feel free to work with the Choir as long as he felt able to do so.

Boris Ord was given the title Director of Music at this time. After I succeeded him, the titles Organist and Director of Music were gradually merged, so that the College now refers to the Organist and Director of Music.

Memories of my years as Organist are legion, many of them of a trifling nature, but nevertheless securely stored. I remember asking a boy who came for audition (was it Andrew Marriner?) how old he was. The reply came back without hesitation: 'I'm eight, sir. How old are you?'

I remember too the day when I came down to conduct the anthem wearing a red cassock, whilst the choir members were (correctly) wearing black cassocks. I tried in vain to conceal the red cassock beneath the surplice which had cut-away arms, but sensing my embarrassment, both choristers and choral scholars found great difficulty in suppressing their giggles, with the result that we only managed to have a quorum for the responses and three Amens. [Both Philip Ledger and Stephen Cleobury can remember a service at which they too appeared (wrongly) in red cassocks!]

As we mark this year the centenary of Boris Ord's birth in 1897, I cannot help thinking how proud and pleased he would be to know of the current standing of the King's College Choir under the leadership of Stephen Cleobury.

## *Philip Ledger, O. & D. of M. 1974-82*

My first visit to King's was as a schoolboy on a misty winter's afternoon. In the candlelit Chapel, Choral Evensong was conducted by Boris Ord, an awesome figure who barely moved his hands yet effortlessly shaped the music with superb artistry and musicality. Later he taught me, as did his successor Sir David Willcocks, a choral conductor with extraordinary insight and skill.

Perhaps what all Directors of Music at King's have instinctively understood is that this marvellous building gives an extra dimension to the music being performed. Perfect intonation, ensemble and phrasing are rewarded and enhanced by an acoustic aura which is recognised throughout the world as 'the King's sound'.

Today this fine tradition is being carried forward splendidly by my successor Stephen Cleobury, who is adding to the reputation of the Choir with the introduction of imaginative new repertoire.

As with cathedral choirs throughout the country, the day begins with an early morning practice at the Choir school. Woe betide any Director of Music who is not fully awake! The choristers will rapidly ensure that this is rectified. Scales and vocal exercises are followed by a rehearsal of the day's music and of the pieces which may be due for performance several days or even weeks ahead. The choristers are all exceptionally gifted musicians and the practice quickly proceeds past the mere learning of notes to questions of interpretation.

Before Evensong the choristers join the choral scholars in Chapel for a full rehearsal when the Director of Music is able to put the final touches to unaccompanied pieces and adjust the balance in music with organ accompaniment.

The daily singing of services gives the Choir its unique quality and strength. The discipline and confidence which result are to be heard in the *Festival of Nine Lessons and Carols*, broadcast live each Christmas Eve.

On the evening before Christmas Eve, I used to hear each of the 16 choristers sing the first verse of *Once in Royal David's City*. The boys did not know who would be chosen to sing this famous solo until about two minutes before the service. We were then already robed and assembled under the organ screen. One year I signalled to a certain boy and two stepped forward! Happily the matter was resolved amicably within seconds before the BBC's red light indicated that we were 'on the air'.

During vacations the Choir regularly undertakes tours to different parts of the world. In 1976, during the American Bicentennial celebrations, we provided the resident Choir for the Convention of the American Guild of Organists in Boston. In 1978 we visited Japan for the first time, giving a series of concerts at a girls' college in Tokyo where the choristers were fêted like pop stars. Autographs were sought and the boys preened themselves as screams of delight from the Japanese girls accompanied the Choir's exit from the hall after performances. Another memorable part of this tour was a visit to Hiroshima where, on a sweltering day in the World Peace Chapel, we sang Purcell's *Remember not, Lord, our offences*. Then in 1980 we undertook a coast-to-coast tour of Australia which culminated in an unforgettable recital in the Sydney Opera House.

Recordings form an important part of the Choir's diary. I remember in particular Bach's *Christmas Oratorio* with Elly Ameling, Dame Janet Baker, Robert Tear and Dietrich Fischer-Dieskau as the soloists. In the middle of an exceptionally harsh winter, Fischer-Dieskau sent a message before the recording sessions saying he hoped we would ensure that Cambridge was warm!

The King's College Choir has an international reputation which is unequalled, and former choristers and choral scholars look back with tremendous gratitude and affection on their time at the College. I wish the Choir and its Director of Music every success in the years ahead.

**91** The three living Organists and Directors of Music combined in February 1983 to perform the Concerto in C for three harpsichords by J. S. Bach, as part of a concert in aid of the Chapel appeal. Photograph: Mick Moore.

*Stephen Cleobury, O. & D. of M. 1982-*

When I was a small child my father practised as a doctor in St Ives, near Cambridge. My mother recalls the occasion when she accidentally shut my hand in the car door outside King's Chapel during a shopping expedition. Supposing I had sustained a permanent injury … Little did we know then how important Cambridge would become for me.

I came up as Organ Student to St John's College in 1967 and had four wonderful years working under George Guest. During this period I played the King's organ for the first time at an Ely Diocesan Choral Festival which David Willcocks was conducting. He told me that the two most important stops were the choir-to-great coupler and the 8-foot pedal flute, the use of which enabled one to hear clearly what one was doing! This advice has served me well. I first conducted in the Chapel at a service sung jointly by the choirs of King's and St John's in 1970, when George Guest was away.

Before moving to King's I directed the choir at Westminster Cathedral, where, as an Anglican in a Roman Catholic church, I was welcomed with great warmth. How, I wondered, would a Johnian be received in King's? My last big Westminster service was the Mass celebrated by the Pope in the summer of 1982. I was delighted to receive a card after this from the choral scholars, who said they had watched the service on television, had enjoyed the music, and were looking forward to working with me.

A few visits to see Philip Ledger followed. He was kindness itself in briefing me for the job, and I arrived in September outwardly prepared, but inwardly nervous.

Nobody could become Director of Music at King's without being acutely aware of the weight of tradition, and the degree of public expectation. Moreover, there was the whole College side to things. I need not have worried on that score, for although people might imagine that such an august institution must be a formal and forbidding place, I soon discovered that King's is an especially lively, liberal and friendly community. I received great support from everyone, not least from David Willcocks and Philip Ledger, my two predecessors, from whom I was lucky enough to inherit such a wonderful musical instrument.

The major blot on my first term was the loss of my brand new bicycle, a leaving present from the chorister parents at Westminster Cathedral. The police advised me to replace it with an old second-hand one, less attractive to burglars. This I did, and it is still with me after 15 years. I remember this means of locomotion being unfavourably compared with the Rolls Royce driven by the leader of the ECO as we both went down West Road one day on the way to a recording session in Chapel!

In any job people spend time doing things they didn't expect to have to do. Media interviews, particularly on tour, fall into this category, and often present tricky moments! I was appearing on a live news bulletin with one of our counter-tenors, when he was asked: 'Now, you're still singing alto at the age of twenty-one: when is your voice going to break?'. On another occasion one of my interlocutors wanted to know: 'what sort of a song is Evensong?'.

It is often the choristers, however, who make the more interesting observations. One likened his time in the Choir to joining a train on part of its long journey: 'you get on at one station and off a little further down the line: you become a small part of a long tradition.' This is a good way to look at my role, too. It helps to keep things in proportion. Most important, amidst all the excitement of tours, recordings and the like, is to help the Choir to do what the Founder intended: to adorn the daily praise of God with beautiful music. Not all choristers have such a philosophical turn of mind. Another, tragically killed in a road accident in his first year at university, had such a charming way of saying things that he shouldn't have said, that he frequently got away with it. Referring to the coat I often wore to morning practice, he said once: 'Sir, why do you always wear that dirty old green mac?'. That stopped me being too serious about everything.

*Christopher Brunelle, c.s. 1989-91*

## The First American Choral Scholar

As the first American to join the Choir, I had a few extra things to learn. In the Congregational church where I grew up, we had never sung psalms; almost all of the settings of the *Magnificat* and *Nunc dimittis* were unfamiliar, and even the responses and many of the hymns were new to me. My two years at King's were thus a thorough and marvellous education in British choral music. I also learned the correct pronunciation of 'water'; before coming to Cambridge I apparently had only been getting the first letter right. But although each of us came to King's with a different and extensive musical background, the most fundamental training that we received there came simply from the daily routine of the Choir and its constant demand for excellence. We were required to give our best every day, no matter how we felt: we learned to overcome colds, the effect of Saturday night upon Sunday morning, discomfort (the Chapel went without heat for a week one cold January: beautiful puffs of steam came from our mouths as we sang), and the other demands of our schedules (essays, exams, extra concerts). In short, we learned to be professional.

We also learned not to be blasé. We never knew on any given day whether choir alumni or other musicians would attend the service, but it was in fact more important to give our best for anyone who might be listening, choral connoisseur or not. This was of course the only decent way to prepare for Christmas Eve, when *everybody* listens; but it was also a reminder that the gift of making music at King's was meant to be shared not only with other musicians but with anyone who cared to listen. We were once rehearsing Fauré's *Requiem* and had just come in the *Agnus Dei* to that simple, sudden, and lovely harmonic shift from C to A flat. We knew the piece well and sang through the passage unconcernedly, at which Stephen Cleobury stopped us. He reminded us that our correct pitch and competent phrasing was not enough: we perhaps had sung that phrase many times, but there would always be those who were hearing it for the first time, and it was our job to make that phrase as magical for them as it had been for us when we first heard the Fauré. We sang it again, and it was.

*Gerald Finley, c.s 1980-3*

## Canadian Choral Scholar

The nervous few shuffled from foot to foot as the sherry slopped into our glasses. The Dean and Director of Music shared a joke until everyone had been served. 'Gentlemen, congratulations and welcome to the Choir.' That moment changed my life.

I had been a chorister at St. Matthew's, Ottawa since the age of 10 and when my voice changed continued in the bass section, struggling with a scratchy new range. I found the challenge and friendship completely involving, and had joined the local choral society, chamber choir and provincial youth choir. It was fun, social and emotionally exhilarating.

But here, *here*! This was a dream attained long before I had expected. Serious stuff. The foundation and pinnacle of choral tradition. The records I had heard, Christmas carols, anthems, great choral works. I was now part of it. The internal jubilation was difficult to control. I choked slightly on the sherry. 'I expect you'll get used to it. We haven't much Canadian beer here', quipped the organ scholar.

So began my journey with the pure English choral institution of King's. As part of the Choir, I felt very much at home, the familiar music and service tradition a follow on from my experience in Canada. There were, however a few exceptions in the Lord's Prayer: accent the first syllable of 'trespasses', not the second; remember when not to continue with 'For thine is the kingdom' (why not?). Be alert to which Creed is on, Nicene or Apostles? Wednesdays were men only—no boys. We hoped it was never the 15th day of the month when an interminably long psalm in plainsong was enough to make you gasp for a drink in the bar, which was crowded by the time this evensong was eventually over. As a Canadian, I found the formal language of the services and the celebration in great style of the Christmas and Easter services impressive. These were the serious responsibilities of the Choir. The life of the choral scholar had other elements, however, not quite so serious.

Not being part of the British establishment and not being American always brought some interesting events. I will not forget the seven hour wait on arrival at

**92** David Willcocks rehearses the Choir.
Photograph: Edward Leigh.

Tokyo's Narita Airport, while the rest of the Choir made their way into Tokyo, having been conclusively assured in London that my being with the Choir excused me from having a visa in my Canadian passport, and then the signing of the official apology to the Emperor for this oversight.

For me, besides the Cambridge life of lazy mid-summer term punting down the Cam, the Madrigals on the River, the extraordinary festivities of May Week with balls and concerts, it was Christmas above all which gave me the strongest memories. Carols from childhood records were offered here, in this beautiful building, the reverberation taking the solo boy's voice upwards to that extraordinary ceiling and beyond. Then, after the crowds of congregation, some of those devotees having camped there for several freezing nights in eager anticipation, had left that carol service, which all my relatives in snowy Ottawa could hear along with the millions across the world, we would then sit down to dinner with the Provost, presented with venison or swan (since at a royal institution, swan was permitted to be eaten), and then having had our fill, stagger into the College hall for the traditional game of Balloon Volleyball, with the Provost as referee, Decani versus Cantoris, that is, one side of the choir against the other. To complete our Christmas Eve vigil, we would sing close harmony to the porters at the Porter's Lodge, all of us confined to College during that lonely Christmas night. And to end the evening, a men only service of the first Christmas Eucharist. I wonder how many of my fellow choral scholars really remember clearly those services. To cheer ourselves on Christmas morning we put a few pounds in a kitty so that we could have our own stockings, filled with whatever goodies the designated Santa Claus decided were appropriate … The soggy, sometimes foggy Christmas morning would entail the final Christmas service and then we would head home, which for me meant a journey of some ten hours, arriving late on Boxing Day, trying to understand the shock of snowmen, snowploughs, and post-Christmas realisation that it would be a long time before it all happened again. But it would happen, next year …

*Ian McDonald, c.s. 1981-3*

## An Australian in Cambridge
In some ways it was a strange meeting for an Australian having grown up in a small rural town to arrive at King's College, Cambridge.

I had been prepared for the world of church music from an early age as a chorister in the town's provincial Cathedral, in a choir that was inspired by the sounds and images of King's as they came to us from the other side of the world. But I had not any warning of the myriad of little (some not so!) social and cultural expectations—games and tests—well rehearsed rituals to be played out before and around me like symphonies of clashing worlds.

I would have to say that through all this my fellow choral scholars were a grounding and stabilising presence for me—a wonderful bunch who delighted in my difference (as they did of other foreign scholars), encouraging me never to merge, for the sake of conformity alone, into the prevailing colours Cambridge so vividly displays. Perhaps even that had its fair share of amusement when it fell my turn to read the lesson at Evensong—or as they would quote to me afterwards with great hilarity—the liss'n.

Cambridge for me seemed a forest of gaffes and triumphs—some real, some only perceived. At my first 'Pre-prandial Society' meeting, when asked with incredulity why I hadn't read Chekov or Keats, and consequently, what I had been doing with my time, my reply was naively, but truthfully, this:

'Just on dusk, the sun low and the air shedding its warmth, one can throw a fist-sized clod across a freshly ploughed and dry paddock, and marvel at its little puff of dust which, back lit by the setting sun, hangs in the cooling air for what seems an

**93** Prince Charles surrounded by the Choir at a Youth and Music concert held at the Royal Academy in London. Photograph: Roger Holmes.

74

eternity. Hours are spent contemplating, judging and delighting in the beauty of each clod, its flight and its far away, silent explosion. This ritual repeated will weave a translucent blanket of dust-mist low across mourning the loss of the day.'

After a slight pause my audience had to concede that this was, in fact, not unlike reading Chekov.

*Georg Ruhland, c.s. 1993-4*

### A German's Year in King's College Choir

It is two years ago now that I left the Choir after having studied law at King's for one year in order to obtain an L.L.M. (postgraduate) degree. Since then, there has not been a day on which I have not been thinking about the Choir.

It will be hardly credible to anyone whose mother tongue is English that there are people that do not know of the existence, let alone the outstanding quality of King's College Choir. But then, the *Festival of Nine Lessons and Carols* which gives the Choir its world-wide popularity and fame, is not yet well-known on the continent—something I am already trying to change, within my possibilities, of course.

Thus, I arrived at King's in October 1993 without really knowing what it was that was expected of me, although my audition not so long before including my first visit to a King's Evensong had given me *some* idea. Additionally, I had been sent the usual letter by the senior choral scholar introducing me to customs and habits of the group, as well as outlining the duties of the Choir. Amongst other things, it was suggested to purchase a gown for use in Chapel. Not aware of the fact that gowns are the most common garments of English church or chapel choirs, it took about two days until I realised that there is nothing peculiar about wearing it.

But this is not really what keeps me thinking of King's every day. To be quite honest, the first couple of months were demanding almost too much of me: neither had I sung even one single English psalm in my life before, nor did I know any of the pieces that we sung up to about Christmas, when some German music first appeared on the schedule. Never before had I experienced a discipline so strict (and in the end: so rewarding), hardly ever had I sung and spoken English so much as I had to do now. Even the Latin which I had expected to be familiar and some 'relief', was suddenly pronounced in an entirely different manner, thereby presenting itself a rather new language to me. In short, I just did not feel up to the very high requirements of the Choir. In the following weeks, though, I increasingly managed to organise my studies and other few activities around the Choir timetable, and I found that the services that I had to prepare thoroughly from day to day got more and more enjoyable. I was allowed to experience the greatest variety of music imaginable to a choir singer and came across all those English composers of whom I had *not* heard before like H. Howells. So, when I am asked today: 'how does Dyson in D go again?', I know. Not many Germans can claim *that*, I take it.

Very often, though, it was not the music on its own but also the—mainly liturgical—setting in which it was performed which made the experience complete. Thus, if given the difficult task to write down my personal 'highlights of the year' I would have to start with the Tallis *Lamentations* on Good Friday. My parents who were present at the time were just as moved as I was and keep speaking of the service until today. For the collectors of more entertaining information it might be worth mentioning that this very emotion took me so far that I once apologised to the Director of Music for a wrong note that someone else had sung. Almost *ex aegno* with this service I would put the *Festival of Nine Lessons and Carols*. Why this was so uplifting hardly needs explanation since most of you probably know from personal—be it radio or live—experience. Furthermore there were, *inter alia*, the European Tour in summer '94 which provides all sorts of remarkable memories, and the grand recording and performance of Bach's *St Matthew Passion* in which the Choir did extremely well with regard to its German pronunciation. So did I, less surprisingly.

I must not forget, finally, to emphasise how much fun I had singing in 'Collegium Regale' (The choral scholars of King's). Especially those *a capella* pop arrangements gave me much inspiration for my own musical work in the future.

### *Alan Bennett, ch. 1937-41*

During Evensong one weekday in 1939 and in the middle of the Magnificat there was a tremendous bang just behind me. Evidently a lump of stone about the size of half a brick had become dislodged from the roof and crashed onto the choir stalls between two of the tenors. It ended up on the choristers' seats so it is as well that we were singing at the time. Mercifully no one was hurt except for a graze on one of the choral scholars. I think that the whole of Cantoris stopped singing but since Decani were carrying on we soon recovered ourselves and rejoined the singing. Had the incident occurred fifty years later it would be interesting to have heard the views of the inspectors about Health and Safety at work!

Then there was the Carol Service on Christmas Eve either 1939 or 1940. David Willcocks who was then organ scholar had just been called up into the services and Boris Ord was laid low with the 'flu. We choristers had no idea how we were going to have an organist and visualised an unaccompanied Festival.

To our great relief sweet music was filling the Chapel as we arrived about half-an-hour before the broadcast was due to start, but it was not till later that we learned that Henry Ley from Eton had come to our rescue. There had not been a single rehearsal with the organist of the day!

### *Peter Bingham, c.s. 1954-7*

An early recollection is of John Walker smoking a final fag before Evensong and not realising that the discarded stub had lodged in his turn-up. He was the senior bass on Cantoris, so we were all able to witness his final few steps towards the stalls trying to kick out the fire that was burning his leg and emitting sparks and smoke from beneath his cassock. On reaching his place, he disappeared to beat out the flames to a further accompaniment of smoke and sparks. It took three attempts before we were able to make a faltering start on the Introit.

### *H. C. G. Brown, c.s. 1936-9*

A fellow choral scholar (I think it was David Senior) bet me I would not spend a night alone in the Chapel. I said I would certainly not stay all night since I valued

my sleep, but, if his bet still held, I was prepared to spend a couple of hours or so. It was agreed that I would go in at 11pm and stay until 1am next morning.

I obtained the keys, and, without much enthusiasm, set about the enterprise being careful (as I thought) that no one, especially the porters, saw me. It was a dark; moonless night and, of course, no flash light could be used. I thought that sufficient illumination would be available inside the Chapel from the town lighting filtering through the windows.

I had not bargained for the velvet blackness of the vast, silent Chapel so I waited a few moments to allow my eyes and nerves to adjust. I then set off slowly up the nave towards the organ loft. About half way to it, I felt I was not alone. Turning, I made out a vague, black shape some way behind me moving noiselessly and slowly towards me.

In those days, I had a particularly lethal right hook, and I advanced upon the shape with speed and purpose. Only when I was a few yards from it did I hear a hoarse whisper: 'for God's sake, it's only me'. It was, of course, my friend making sure that I was carrying out my part of the bet. What I said was not entirely appropriate to the premises though it was, perhaps, to the occasion. However, bet or no bet, I was glad of his company.

We then decided to carry out an experiment. Whilst I remained at the altar, my friend would walk to the other end of the Chapel. We synchronised our watches (fortunately they were luminous) and within an agreed span of five minutes, he would make a sound—source unknown to me—and I would note the time and describe it—if I could hear it.

Just as I was beginning to think the whole thing farcical, I suddenly heard, quite distinctly, a tinkling sound. I noted the time and made my way down the Chapel. I told my friend what I thought I had heard and the time, and he confirmed both. What I could not say was what I thought had caused the sound. He had, he said, dropped a small pin.

As far as I know, that pin may still be there: it was too small to consider retrieving in the dark. In any case, I had had enough and was glad to get to bed.

*Sir David Calcutt, c.s. 1950-4*

**At the Customs**

Whilst on tour in Switzerland, Boris bought a most expensive new Swiss watch. As such, it was dutiable on return to the UK. Boris made elaborate precautions to defeat the Revenue. 'As we pass through customs', Boris explained to an unwilling choral scholar, 'you will ask me the time, and I will say that I am afraid I do not have a watch.' As a side-show, he arranged that one of the choristers should release a hydrogen balloon, in the customs shed, just as Boris was about to reach the customs officer, and that the chorister would create an enormous disturbance to distract the officer's attention. Unfortunately when the great moment arrived Boris forgot some of the arrangements he had carefully made. The choral scholar dutifully asked him the time but he, distracted by the release of the hydrogen balloon, elaborately got out his new watch from his deepest pocket and announced the time. 'Excuse me sir', enquired the customs officer, 'did you buy that watch whilst you were in Switzerland?'

*John Carol Case, c.s. 1941-2 and 1945-7*

All the medieval stained-glass in the Chapel was removed for safety during the war, the windows being covered with roofing felt.

**95**  Boris Ord after the Honorary Degree ceremony, at the Senate House, 1960. Photograph: Rowe Library.

I was lucky enough to return to King's in October 1945, and early in 1946 the task of cleaning and replacing the glass began. Although nearly fifty years ago, I can still remember going into Chapel one morning and finding that first panel which had been restored to the East window with the sun shining through: it shone like a jewel, and was a wonderful assurance that peace had fully returned.

*Chris Chivers, c.t. 1989-94*

✧

A few years ago I was preparing a group of choristers for Confirmation, when I asked if anyone knew the word beginning with 'A' for a person not at all sure about their belief in God. The group looked rather baffled, but after a delay of a few moments one chorister supplied the correct answer. 'Agnostic, sir.' So then I asked if anyone knew the word, also beginning with 'A', for a person who didn't believe in God at all. A hand immediately shot up: 'Anglican, sir!'

*Roger Firkins, c.s. 1946-50*

✧

Although by the late 1940s Boris had become quite mellow, there were moments of friction in the Choir, normally with the late Kenneth Long who was already over thirty, a very good musician, but not a great singer (almost as bad as Boris himself!).

Boris was always getting at Kenneth in Choir practices until one evening Kenneth could stand it no longer. To our horror, he stormed out, thrusting his music on Boris's desk with the words, 'Here you, sing it yourself!'. An attempt at reconciliation later that evening is reputed to have ended with them hurling the English Hymnal at each other. Nevertheless there was some kind of armed truce and Kenneth continued in the Choir.

The sequel took place at the next Lammas Day Breakfast. We had decided that Boris needed a new dressing gown. (There were no bathrooms in Gibbs in those days and Boris tottering over to Webb's Court in his disreputable and threadbare dressing gown at about 10am was one of the sights of Cambridge.) When the lengthy meal was over, we duly gave B.O. his present, with which he was delighted; but there was a sting in the tail—or rather the pocket—a little book by Kenneth Long called 'Church Choir Management'. Happily, Boris was even more delighted.

*G.H. 'Sandy' Forsyth, ch. 1930-6: c.s. 1939-42*

✧

**Chorister chores**

Music for the practices at the Choir School (two per day) had to be lugged up after Evensong, and of course returned next day. I use the word lugged because it was all in bound volumes. Volumes I & II were rarely used, if ever, but Vol III, the heaviest and very large (Walmisley services chiefly), was, and it fell to the lot of the three most junior (and the smallest!) to carry them. The more senior you were, the lighter the book you carried. It was at least three years before loose scores were introduced and I remember a piece by Herbert Howells, whose music we had just started to sing, was one of the first—in an orange folder.

**The Vice-Provost's Christmas present**

There is one tradition that must surely still be in existence and that is the Christmas present left to the choristers by some kind benefactor. It was worth 5s. but rose to 7s. 6d. by the time I left. It must have risen further over the years. It was given to us on Christmas morning by the Vice-Provost who also presented us with a book of our own choice. Vice-Provost Sheppard always signed the fly-leaf.

**96** Roy Goodman conducting the School's junior orchestra. Photograph: King's College School.

I still treasure the six books I received during my time as a chorister. [This tradition is still in existence today.]

*Peter Godfrey, ch. 1931-6; c.s. 1941-2 & 45-6; acting O. & D. of M. 1978*

During the 1930s many of the parents who had boys in the Choir were quite poor. My father had to borrow money from a cousin of his to pay my fees. But the sort of general training which choristers get … concentration, discipline etc … must have stood us in good stead for the future. Three other exact contemporaries of mine (who got into the Choir in 1931) were all in similar circumstances … but, I suppose, all of us made it in the end. One became a Major General in the Army, and was knighted, another became head of the Eastern Region of the British Railways, the third became Professor of Dutch at the University of Hull, and I was the fourth. [Peter Godfrey went on to a distinguished career as a professor and conductor in New Zealand.]

*Roy Goodman, ch. 1959-64*

### Choristers on the Roof
I recall a choristers' visit to go up and walk on the Chapel's vaulted roof. At the time Simon Preston was recording an LP of Messiaen on the organ, and of course when we discovered a little peep-hole in the roof directly above the organ loft it was too tempting not to push a little bit of soot through. This did not go down so well with Simon and I recall his voice bellowing out a loud reproach!

### The recording of Allegri's *Miserere*
The Allegri has two little stories, I suppose, but unfortunately no ROYalties! I am sure that Michael George and I were late for the recording session in the chapel because we had been playing in a rugby match. We hadn't bothered to really shower and so ran to chapel with muddy knees under our long trousers. We discovered that the Choir was already singing and David Willcocks was trying out various boys to sing the solo. It got to my turn and he decided that I was in good form and so we started recording what has turned out to be this 'angelic' Allegri *Miserere* (muddy knees and all!). We also sang it, of course, at the Ash Wednesday service, and quite often it was sung by more than one boy. There was a friendly old man who used to write in to David Willcocks and enquire the name of the boy soloist so that he could send him a congratulatory letter and a book token. Of course Mr Willcocks used to reply that actually it was more than one boy. As luck would have it, the year I sang it solo, the same man wrote in to enquire the names of the boys! Since then it seems to haunt me all over the world—I have dined out on it in Australia, Japan and the USA. I had a student on teaching practice once who almost wanted to wash my feet when he discovered who I was!

At university he had run a seance group and their meeting had begun with this atmospheric recording. I know that Rowan Atkinson, amongst others, chose to take it to his desert island, and more recently John Peel chose it during an interview on Radio 3, adding the comment 'I wonder what that angelic little boy is doing now—he's probably a second-hand car salesman in Basingstoke!' At this point Michael Berkeley made an attempt to put him right!

*Brian Head, c.s. 1955-9*

In 1955 when I came up as a choral scholar … regular tours and concert work were yet to become part of the King's way of life, and so it was that a performance of Fauré's *Requiem* and the Schütz *Christmas Story* with the Philharmonia Orchestra, when Denis Brain played the french horn in motoring gloves to counteract the frigidity of the Chapel, and the film for the old British Transport Films called 'The England of Elizabeth', were momentous occasions for us. The latter was the last film-score Vaughan Williams, then well over eighty years of age, wrote and the images of King's and the Choir with Boris moving slowly behind us in procession in glorious technicolour are treasured to this day. The film was screened by Channel 4 a decade ago, and is the last performing image of Boris with his Choir to remain.

97   A scene from the television documentary 'The England of Elizabeth', filmed in 1956. Photograph: Anon.

The wonders of modern recording aids had not been fully developed in the second half of the '50s, but simple, if unwieldy, reel-to-reel machines did exist, and thanks to my close contemporary school friend Roger Martin, a King's history scholar, a small microphone was lodged behind the wooden fretwork above the choir stalls on Decani with a lead over the organ, into the then choristers' vestry, and through into the side chapel beyond. Here Roger's Grundig [a tape recorder] was lodged for a year and a half, and while Boris often commented on 'those funny wires', and the operator came and went like the invisible man, many services were safely recorded. Most contemporary choral scholars and chorister parents will have privately made LPs of the best of these recordings, and in fact Boris was presented with copies of services that we knew would give him joy in those sad last days in his rooms over the Jumbo Arch.

*Alastair Hume, c.s. 1962-5*

David Willcocks was very worried about the prospect of some chaps the King's Singers throwing themselves into the vicissitudes of the life of a touring musician. He generally tended to advise against it, saying that Simon Carrington and I were half-decent double-bass players and that we should stick to something we could (sort of!) do. This may also have been connected with the fact that David did actually call me, to my face, '...the worst alto we've ever had in this Choir'. We were rehearsing Byrd's *Second Service*, I think it was, and the Cantoris alto part is fairly unforgiving at one point, being a succession of fourths and fifths just to make the harmony work. David quickly identified where the bum notes were coming from, made me sing it on my own, and then pronounced the judgement on me.

The Choir always put a boat on the river for the May Bumps [rowing races]. Five out of the six original King's Singers took up an oar for the glory of the College. When the four-minute warning gun was fired, the whole eight would sing *Forth in thy name, O Lord, we row*, before jumping into the boat ready for the start. If we made a bump we would immediately pull over and sing *Cantate Domino*. If, on the other hand, we got bumped, we would pull over and sing *Drop, drop, slow tears*. It's funny but we had lots of performances of *Drop, drop, slow tears* that year.

One of the college waiters was called Mr. Ship. He spotted pretty early on in my time at King's that I had an Achilles' heel—custard. In 1979 at the annual

conference of the Incorporated Society of Musicians, Sir David Willcocks, as President, had invited us back to entertain after dinner. It was a fairly august crowd, and we were just finishing one of our most ravishing numbers with the audience eating out of the palms of our hands, when I became aware of this figure threading its way between the tables and heading straight for us. He bore in his hand a large pudding-bowl filled to the brim with custard, together with a spoon, and announced to the startled and assembled company that this was a ceremonial bowl of custard specially created by Chef for the moment. I had no option but to take a few spoonfuls on board there and then, after which there was definitely an added warm, glutinous quality to the voice for the remainder of our musical offering. That occasion was marked by a photograph featuring Sir David, the President of the Society, and Ian Wallace, the President-elect, perched quite a long way up King Henry VI in the Front Court, with the King's Singers, and Philip Ledger, the then Organist and Director of Music, ranged at their feet.

98 David Willcocks, Philip Ledger, Ian Wallace and the King's Singers on the fountain in chapel court following the dinner referred to in Alastair Hume's reminiscence. Photograph: Edward Leigh.

*Brian Kay, c.s. 1962-5*

Standing directly opposite me in the choir stalls was a counter-tenor who taught me how to raise my right hand with confidence whenever I sang a wrong note—just to let the Director of Music know that I knew I'd done it! His hand seemed to be permanently raised. He was Alastair Hume, and we were to spend the next twenty years making music together in the King's Singers. It's not that he made more mistakes than anyone else. He was just more honest—then he was reading Law!

But those who work hard deserve to play hard too—and we did! We choral scholars were at College all the time—even at Christmas. We were in the privileged position of being able to develop close friendships with the College staff—those who so wonderfully looked after our every need—in the dining hall, the 'bedders', and the porters.....One of our number was discovered walking through the College at 2 o'clock one morning escorting a young lady (who went on to become a very famous singer!) through the College grounds—unforgivable in those (relatively) disciplined days. The porter—the wonderful Wilfred—simply looked at the young lady in question, froze for a moment in disbelief, and then uttered the immortal line: 'you can't wear skirts in here, sir!'.

Rumour has it that Al Hume and I went to ask David Willcocks if the idea of an all-male group (or 'all-male grope' as one famous misprint had it!) was a good one. DVW apparently suggested that it would never work, which is why we agreed to stay together for only two and a half years! Nearly thirty years later—in June 1996—I proudly stood on the platform of St David's Hall in Cardiff and presented a concert by the current King's Singers (the Grandchildren, as we call them), and it was heart-warming to discover how wide of the mark that original prediction had been!

99 Philip Ledger surrounded by the Choir, holding up a golden disc awarded for the sale of over one million records by EMI. Photograph: © EMI Records Ltd.

*Pat Magee, ch. 1924-9; c.s. 1934-9; chaplain 1946-52*

**First broadcast of Carol Service**
It was on Christmas Eve 1928 that the BBC first broadcast the Carol Service. I recorded thus in my diary: 'Practise 10-12.45. Go out to dinner with Mum and Dad. Carol Service broadcasted [sic]. Comes off well. I read a lesson and sing a solo in *Lullay*. Dean's party in Beves' room.' A typical boy's matter-of-fact record of an event which we never suspected at the time would one day become a regular part of the national scene.

**Choir Tour abroad**
The second foreign tour which the Choir made took us to Belgium in 1949. Looking back over the years it is difficult to recapture the experience of arriving in a city where food was plentiful, while rationing at home was still at its highest. All were anxious to take back some luxury unobtainable in England. The boys, under instruction from their parents, specialised in liqueur chocolates. But they bought so much loot that they had to sit on their suitcases in order to shut them. Alas, on arrival home the opening of the cases revealed pyjamas and underclothes glued by a sticky substance which permeated the luggage.

100    This choir photograph taken in 1941 shows two Directors of Music, Harold Darke, seated fourth from the left, and Boris Ord, seated fourth from the right, in his R.A.F. uniform. Dean Milner-White sits between them. Photograph: Hill & Saunders.

*Anthony Musson, c.s. 1985-8*

**1986 Tour to East and West Germany and Finland**
While staying in West Berlin we were scheduled to take a trip to East Berlin and give a concert in the evening. A week or so previously a lorry with its front end reinforced with concrete had rammed its way through Checkpoint Charlie and its occupants had escaped to the West. The border guards were now understandably nervous, especially of large vehicles and unusual parties. The sniffer dogs came on board our coach and the twitchy guards threatened to take away my camera when I took a photo of the Checkpoint position.

After a tour of the city by coach we were allowed out on foot to visit the tomb of their Unknown Soldier. One of the choristers edged out his camera to take a picture of the grave and the eternal flame beside it. Immediately the guard raised his gun at the astonished boy and looked for all the world as though he would have shot him if Gerald Peacocke had not hurriedly convinced the now traumatised boy to desist. Approaching the British Ambassador's residence for lunch we noticed the watchers in their cars and were told by embassy staff that even the movements of the dogs were recorded.

Our programme was, I seem to remember, almost totally unaccompanied and included among other things four Magnificats and the John Browne *Stabat Mater*. No matter how esoteric, the concert was a great success. It was followed by refreshments in the crypt and an extremely moving speech by a musician (connected with the church?) who so wished that they were able to get to other countries to tour or hear beautiful music. From our extremely brief visit we were able to appreciate in some small measure the restrictions and longings which the people in the Soviet bloc were forced to endure. The day after was a free day and we spent time wandering round the Checkpoint Charlie Museum and tracing the patterned enormity of the Berlin Wall. Little did we realise that their and our past experiences would soon become a thing of the past.

*Jim Peschek, c.s. 1943-4 & 1946-9*

A BBC recording session late one Friday evening. University Church bell ringers were in full spate as usual and this inconvenience had been forgotten about in the

planning. A messenger was sent over to ask for their consideration but couldn't make contact. Garth Benson (the then organ scholar) was sent over but returned unsuccessful.

Then Boris Ord (University Organist) decided to take matters in hand. The ringers had locked themselves in the belfry (as usual) and were virtually inaccessible. Boris headed for the mains electric switch and cut off the current, plunging the belfry into darkness. It certainly produced the right result. I don't think the ringers ever knew who did it. The recording went ahead with no further difficulties.

### Simon Preston, ch. 1949-52; o.s. 1958-61

By 1961, when I was in my last year as organ scholar at King's, Boris had become quite infirm and was confined to his splendid set of rooms in the Gibbs Building. At this point I was in two minds as to whether or not I should stay on for a further year to sit the Bachelor of Music (Mus.B.) exam and Boris must somehow have got wind of this for he asked me to call on him; concerned that I might make a mistake I would later regret, he suggested a bargain. If I stayed at King's, sat the Mus.B., and passed it first time, he would give me his own Mus.B. hood, which I was led to understand had been given to him by the one-time Cambridge Professor of Music, Sir Charles Villiers Stanford. Certainly the hood itself looked as though it had been owned by others even before Stanford, but, as this was an offer I could hardly refuse, I did stay the extra year, passed the degree first time, and duly received the by now splendidly restored hood, which I still proudly possess.

### Patrick Robertson, ch. 1922-8; c.s. 1932-5

**101** The Choir with Boris Ord in 1956. Photograph: R.B.C. Wagg.

**Whit-Monday treat**
In those days (1922-8) Whitsun was a special occasion, and on Whit-Mondays all the choristers were invited by the College to climb the one hundred or so steps onto the roof of the Chapel. School staff came with us and so did 'Daddy' Mann in his late seventies. When we had exhausted the views and had penetrated the inner roof, thick with pigeon droppings (!), Mann invited us all into the organ loft. For the most junior boys this was a thrill because for them 'the organ' was out of bounds.

When we were all squashed in we were asked what we would like to sing. The immediate and unanimous response was *Let the bright seraphim*. So we sang, fortissimo, Mann finishing off with a fine flourish on the organ. He turned and chuckled with pleasure. While I was a chorister this became an annual celebration for Whit-Monday.

### Robert Tear, c.s. 1957-60

My memory of King's Choir started with the following conversation:
    B. Ord: 'Have you had any singing lessons Mr. Tear?'
    R. Tear: 'No sir.'
    B. Ord: 'Good. In that case you won't ruin my choir.'
After that rather disconcerting beginning, my experience in the Choir was one approaching sublimity. The music, candles, glass are now fused as magic in my present recollection.

## Rodney Williams, ch. 1952-5

### Boris and the powercuts

Organ cuts out in full practice. Boris:'Mr McLean will you go and ring the power station and tell them I must have the organ for Evensong.'—off goes Hugh McLean, returning from the Porter's Lodge,'I'm sorry, Boris, there's nothing they can do.'—Boris Ord:'Very well, I shall have to go myself!'—storms off leaving Hugh McLean to take over the rehearsal—returns a while later beaming—'Gentlemen, I have spoken to the power station and we shall have the organ in time for the service.'

### The last 78 r.p.m. recording

Boris, listening to playback of a 'take'—'What's that filthy noise on the bass line!?' … one bold choral scholar—'I'm afraid that's you, Boris, singing.'—pause: B. O. 'Oh!!!—why didn't you tell me?—now we shall have to do it again!'

### B. O.

Whilst I was at King's an advert for Life-buoy toilet soap came out with the slogan 'Protect yourself against B. O.' (One often referred to him by his initials and he himself used them to great effect!) A mischievous choral scholar cut one of these out of a magazine and pinned it on the choristers' notice board in our vestry. We were half afraid of the reaction it might provoke, but need not have feared, Boris saw it and laughed till he cried.

**102** Philip Ledger with the choristers outside the Chapel. Photograph: Unknown.

## Jonathan Rippon, c.s. 1992-5

I was privileged in my time as a choral scholar to sing the solo part in *Rise, Heart!*, one of Vaughan Williams' *Five Mystical Songs,* from the organ loft overlooking the Chapel, Choir and congregation. This was definitely a high-point, in every sense of the word. Singing from that position gives an added exhilaration to a piece of music which is already incredibly uplifting. Esoteric memories like this are balanced by some amusing, more 'down-to-earth' reminiscences.

One time the Choir was singing *The Lamentations of Jeremiah* by Thomas Tallis (an unaccompanied piece) up at the altar-end of the Chapel in front of the beautiful Rubens painting. The performance was going extremely well, and you could sense that everyone had that magical feeling of being transported to another world that happens in special performances. Suddenly a tourist in the congregation seated near to the altar took a photograph (never allowed in a service) with a large flash, which was momentarily blinding. That would have been bad enough, but it was obviously the last shot on that film, because her camera went onto automatic rewind very loudly throughout the rest of the piece!

Another frustrating occurrence happened quite regularly after the choral scholars had sung a 'Men's voices only' service, i.e. with no trebles, who were having a rest-day. We were leaving the Chapel along with members of the congregation only to overhear one person say to another, 'Of course, that wasn't the *real* King's College Choir.' The choristers get quite enough publicity and attention in the normal course of things, so a comment like that can really make a choral scholar's blood boil!

*All these reminiscences, and indeed the book as a whole, demonstrate that, no matter which era of the Choir's history he was part of, everyone remembers his association with the Choir with great fondness and pride. We hope that this book gives an insight into what it feels like to be part of the unique choral tradition that is the King's College Choir.*

**103** The Choir's recording of Handel's *Messiah* won a Hollywood Golden Angel Award for the best classical music video of 1995. Stephen Cleobury is seen here receiving the trophy and certificate from Hans Petri of Columns Classics. Photograph: Penny Cleobury.

# INDEX